Designed, organized and printed by:
Update Plus
Skra 1-3, Athens 176 73 Greece
Tel.: 30-1-9570396, Fax: 30-1-9573923
Email: update@otenet.gr

Edited by: Mary McFadden

Book Cover design and photograph organization by: Angela Straga
and Amalia Decca

To Order book:
Contact: Website: www.geocities.com/uponthesea/index.html
          Email: uponthesea@yahoo.com
 or write: Joyce Gleeson-Adamidis (Book Order)
            5640 Puite Ct.
            Mariposa, CA 95338 USA

DEDICATIONS

To my husband who has never believed it would happen.

To Admiral Angelos Argyropoulos for his confidence in me
and his gracious help.

To Mom, Dad, Haris, David, Karen, Donald, Patty, Sharon and Amalia
for unconditional love and support.

To my Editor, Mary McFadden, for skill and humor.

CONTENTS

Chapter One
The Innocent Aboard

Chapter Two
Changing Shifts-Changing Partners

Chapter Three
Whoops

Chapter Four
'Once In a Lifetimers'

Chapter Five
Those in Peril on the Sea (including me)

Chapter Six
Rule Britanis

Chapter Seven
The Passenger Chronicles

Chapter Eight
The Crew's Nest

Chapter Nine
Comparison Sailing

Chapter Ten
Thanks For Your Memories

Chapter Eleven
Next Deck Please

CONTENTS

Chapter One
The Innocent Aboard

Why am I doing this - resigning as a travel agency manager and moving to a foreign country? I am not defecting from flag or family or friends. I cherish all of them. To leave and learn; to earn a living in a perhaps unconventional way. It all sounded right to me. Athens, Greece sounded like a good place for my odyssey to begin.

I paused at age 35 to review my past adventures. It was enough to frighten any set of parents. I know that now but I was age 23 then. Like Alice, I became "curioser and curioser" and each turn around each corner tempted me to the next. It would eventually lead me to "life at sea." There I would see marine life and human life; each in a fascinating variety. I would live and work with Americans, Greeks, Italians, Canadians, English, Bangladeshis, Caribbeans, Spanish, Chinese, French, Germans, Croatians, Serbs, Irish, and others.

I had taken a group of 200, through my travel agency, on a Panama Canal Cruise. A young Greek was aboard and we began dating. It was a romantic fling on a romantic ship sailing romantic waters. I saw him as often as possible when he was in port. When he telephoned, his voice was sensual and I followed it all the way to Greece. He dared me to come and I did. The language was impossible to decipher. I constantly heard "Yia Sou." Was that one word or two? Should I smile when the locals said it to me?

After we vacationed around the isles of the Aegean, Poros, and Hydra for two blissful weeks, I began looking for work. I ran out of money but not pride. I refused to call home for help. In one week, I again landed a travel agency job escorting groups of Americans around Athens, then, taking them to a ship to continue their vacation. For three weeks I elbowed my way on the crowded buses; inhaled smells of those who didn't know the word "deodorant"; dusted my apartment twice a day from the pollution and dealt with the pushiness of the women at the local farmers' market. I needed civilization. Or, my definition of civilization. Leaving a country so

1

advanced for one so distinctively different, was a constant challenge. Was the culture I adopted so suppressive that it would stifle me? I was searching for completion and knew only that.

Each afternoon the stores and businesses took a three-hour break. This was my time to go back to my apartment for a quick dusting, a snack, an hour of rest and back to the agency or to the airport to pick up some Americans. Without a telephone, and a seven year waiting list to get one, I was unable to call friends or family. I would go to the corner periptero (a kiosk selling cigarettes, candy, newspaper and nick knacks) and use the telephone there. I was trying to get on board the same cruise ship as my Greek boyfriend. I had applied to Sun Line Cruises in Piraeus, Greece. They called me one day and asked me to come to the office the following morning. I was thrilled but nervous because I had no idea of how to work on a ship. There were no training schools and no instructors years ago. I was told, "You'll learn what you have to on board." I was assigned to a ship called the Stella Oceanis, with 300 passengers, 130 crew members and two other women. Given the ratio, this was a woman's paradise. There were Greek gods catering to everyone's wants and needs and offering assistance wherever necessary. (I thought.)

I was never really popular in school. I was a swimmer, band member, worked to pay off my car, and had a few close personal friends. I dated; usually guys six to eight years older than I but I was never goggled at as I was on a ship. The constant attention that is paid to any woman, whatever her size, shape or appearance is guaranteed to lower her resistance." No" becomes "Maybe" and eventually, "Yes". (I know) It was easy to fall into a trap of wanting to sample the entire menu. More than one young man on board put my heartbeat into overtime. Then the moral values my parents instilled would come to the fore. I acted on those values for at least half of the time. My boyfriend and I met once a week, which had to satisfy us until we could go on vacation together.

Alas, in the interim, rumors were flying and they were about me. It was obvious to everyone but me that I was having an affair with each person I talked or laughed with, including the girls. The next week someone else was the subject of conversation and the following week it was another's turn. This ritual never stopped. One day the ship's telephone operator told me all the gossip that was being spread about me. I laughed. Although she was my roommate, I saw very little of her because she spent her evenings with her married boyfriend. The gossips' mentality was simple: Step one was conversation. Step two was sex. I enjoyed visiting exciting places and ignored the stories about my escapades.

There were some characters on board who could send a shiver down my spine. In my early twenties, I didn't have the experience necessary to handle extraordinarily gruesome people. I was warned that I would have a problem with two high-ranking officers. One officer, the Staff Captain, liked his lady friends, while the other one had a mean demeanor that would send waves of fear throughout the ship's personnel - both men and women. He drew his sword against all. He was the Chief Purser. His responsibilities included all monies, salaries, bills and cabin arrangements on board. And in his opinion, to know everybody's business. He had a menacing manner. His craving for malice was impossible to camouflage. His resolute mouth and flashing black eyes had a fixed purpose when he came toward you. My woman's instinct flashed warning signs of the peril lurking around the corner for me.

The second in command, the Staff Captain, is the tough guy. He is the disciplinarian and the one responsible for the safety on board. Not an enviable position but most of them do the best they can. There is always one who is unable to control his superiority complex and needs to subjugate everyone to his will. He was on board. He would try to tempt a woman to bed with every lure he could devise, including deceit. When I tell someone, "No, thank you. I'm flattered but not interested", I expect them to be done with it. Not this one. The chase becomes the game and winning is vital. I would not give in. It was not even a temptation; I already had a man. To the Staff Captain, I was a challenge. I was unaware that my "No" was having such a ripple effect but it was. The more he couldn't have me, the more he verbally abused and harassed everyone else on board. The cruise director, Willy, (God bless his heart) kept telling me to hold my ground. He asked me several times,
"Why don't you notice them?"
"Why should I notice, I wasn't interested."
There were reports of a ship's pool. Who would get me into bed? I never acknowledged that I even knew about the bet but I did hear that the ante was high.

Enough. It was time for a showdown. One night I asked the Staff Captain to get a bottle of wine chilled. I met him in his cabin a few hours later. I drank one glass, turned to him and asked him to remove his clothing. Without any hesitation he undressed and moved his toneless wobbly belly into the bed. I asked him if it was okay to tie him up, because I wanted excitement. He agreed, nodding his head with such enthusiasm it was hard not to roar with laughter. As I tied him up, he was grinning from ear to ear. I knew he was rehearsing how he would spread the word of his victory. He then asked me if I liked candlelight. Sure, why not, his wish was my command. I took out a tall yellow candle from the drawer of his dresser next to the bed. I put it in the holder and lit it. I turned off the lights, leaned over, gave him a big lipstick-red kiss on his forehead and told him to enjoy a peaceful sleep. An hour and a half later, his cabin steward, offering more wine, found him naked and still tied up. From then on, I was never again bothered, harassed or talked about by that officer. In fact, he even helped me out with others who tried to give me a hard time.

I didn't blame the crew for trying. Every week I watched women passengers, even those with husbands on board, sneaking away with a crew member for a romantic interlude. I was shocked. If a woman wanted to have an affair, fine; but on a ship not famous for soundproof cabins, it was pretty chancy. How far away could a husband be on a 300-passenger ship! It was simply part of the Dare game. Even today I am amazed at it but no longer shocked. We on board are also tourists; we are passenger watchers. Our people scenery changes constantly. Who will arrive next? It makes it hard to settle down because you always wonder if something better is going to come along. Yet, after many cruises, loneliness and a certain desperation settles in. There is no special person to cuddle up to or whom you can trust with your inner thoughts - a rare find on land or sea. My innocence was about to be sacrificed to the chaotic life at sea. I could roll with the waves or go against the current.

I was nineteen years old in 1962 when I boarded my first ship. Not on a passenger ship, but a cargo ship. I hated the ship bitterly. I was desperate to leave. There were about thirty men working, what kind of fun is that. I worked for eight months as a server to the crew. We started sailing from Pelos, Greece to Korea and Japan. Bristol, England was our first stop. Little did I know what life was all about at such a young age. Being a man and like most men,

I never sat down and directly thought about how my life has transpired through the years. As they say in English, I just go with the flow. I just accepted the transformation as a natural process, until my wife sat me down one day and asked me about my life.

I settled in a little bit in the routine with the men, but remained a bit reserved. I always have been like this, never feeling the need to boast of my conquests or brag about my accomplishments. I just went along with whatever we were to do. There were perpetual jokes played not only on the new comers, but the old timers as well. Naturally, we all hated to get up in the morning. We would leave our cabin doors open with just a latch hook keeping them from banging against the wall during rough seas. Also, we had to keep those doors open in case of any emergencies to escape fast. Anyway, when the two men came to wake us up in the morning, we had placed buckets of water balanced on the door so that when they were opened all the way, the waterfall fell dead center on them. No, they didn't get angry. They would just get even with us during the course of the next few days.

There is always someone in the group that is known as a little bit of a dummy. Among the Greeks, we pick on those from the island of Chios. They are known to be quite intense, but yet clever in making money in the shipping world. Anyway, I had this one man continuously pushing me to play cards with him. We usually played cards around Christmas and New Years to give us some form of entertainment to pass the time. This guy loved the game thirty-one, I couldn't stand it, and he wanted to play for money. I didn't want to get involved with money. However, I would give in and play. When I was dealing the cards, to myself I would count out twenty-seven or twenty-eight, but tell him he had thirty-one. Every time he would believe me and never count out his cards. He could never figure out how he always lost.

Another time we had a man who just returned to the ship after having a date with a girl. We started harassing him that maybe he will now catch something contagious. He became nervous and scared. I told him about this pill that would help prevent him from catching anything. He eagerly swallowed the pill with a large bottle of water. Later, when he needed to urinate, it came out bright red. He ran out of the cabin screaming his way to the doctor. We fell back laughing ourselves silly.

5

One of the boys hung an icon of St. Nicholas on the wall above his head over the bed. St. Nicholas is the protector of sailors at sea. When he wasn't there or not looking, I would turn the icon about face, particularly when we had very rough seas. At these times it was misery for all, we had to find someway to bear and get through it. When this boy would climb into bed, he would look up at his icon, see that it was turned and would run out of the cabin screaming that we were going to sink or something bad was going to happen, for St. Nicholas was no longer watching over us.

Once we arrived in the port of Bristol, we would race to get our feet on land. When work was finished, we hit the nearest coffee shop, pub or bar looking for girls. There were no discos in those times, but we didn't have to look far. There was always at least one woman around. Sometimes prostitutes or sometimes just a woman who wanted to be with a sailor for whatever her private reasons were for. We ventured out mostly in groups of four. If we didn't find girls, we passed our time having drinks and talking.

Our travel to the next port was Houston, Texas. I didn't like the United States much on my first visit, in fact I hated it, because Immigration would not let the young sailors off, or the ones who were there for the first time. They feared those who wanted to jump the ship. I had to remain on board for the next 30 days. Imagine not being able to get off. I was not thrilled!

We traveled on to Korea and Japan, where I had no problems disembarking. In Korea, I met up with my first oriental woman. We had been talking in the bar with all the other guys and this one girl kept close to me and talking. Eventually she asked me if I wanted to come with her. I went, why not? I was young, looking for adventure and didn't really know what to expect. I left without telling anyone else about it. She took me to a hut type house that she was living in. It was made of tin with a dirt floor. She seductively laid me. To my utter surprise, it didn't take long. My innocence and youth gave me away. I enjoyed it all the same and she seemed to as well. Knowing she was a prostitute, I always wondered why she never asked me for any money. Later we went to Mozi, Japan. Four of us went together to a local bar looking for girls. There was only one girl. I went first and paid at the bar for my time. I went in, however, before ever entering her, my youth once again took hold and I surprised myself again. What's fair is fair. I didn't have her.

6

Why pay for something I didn't get, or something I could do on my own. I looked at her and demanded my money back or she would have to try to get me going again. Hesitating, but finally relenting, she told the barman to refund my money. The other three guys took their turns. However, over the next few days, those three guys got an STD and were really sore with me.

I was beginning now to learn the old cliché of sailors having a woman in every port. We never stayed long in one area, there were no women working on board to forge any kind of relationship, so what were we supposed to do? We were just passing through during a short time. When nature calls, get the job done. For obvious reasons bonding with anyone was nonexistent; life went on its merry way. Since I was about to make ships my life, formulating early in my mind, I wondered what is the reason to get married? It is not fair to a wife to leave her at home, have kids, return home for two to three months a year, then after 35 years retire, returning home to what? Grown up kids I didn't help with and a woman whom I really don't know. This wasn't right for me. At this time, however, I wasn't able to see the final days of my first contract. Like a baby, I hated the cargo ships and wanted to go home.

When the sea was rough, it was really rough. Sometimes it would last 20 or 25 days. Nothing short of torture and hell. Days were endless and nights were longer. Would it end? Could it end? Just let me off. However, once we arrived in port, all the past days were forgotten. Off we'd go to find entertainment on land.

As time passed, we visited more and more ports, thus making it easier and easier for one to learn the art of picking up girls. One time in Savannah, Georgia, we all went out early one afternoon to have a drink. There was only one girl in the bar and one of the men I was with started up a conversation with her. He started teasing her about how the Greeks have a special way. She told him she didn't mind. She turned to me and asked if she could visit the ship. She took me to the ship in her car. There was an old man sleeping in the car, she explained he was her grandfather and they were on their way to some place. She left him there and came on board with me. I took her to my cabin, we did our thing and off she went never looking behind. Me? I fell asleep.

Eat a little, drink a little and womanize a little, this was the motto for free time. Eventually I got used to it and just bided my time. After all, when I finished my first contract, I was obliged to do my military service of two years. What new fresh quest was waiting ahead?

Chapter Two
Changing Shifts - Changing Partners

As we read our romantic adventure novels, we tend to become the heroes of them; assuming their desires, dreams and living their journeys. I, too, have listened for the hoof beat of the white horse, the clanking of the knight's armor and prayed the pair was headed for my castle. Or, a squeaky clean, white-hulled yacht. Any ship inherently carries all the emotions an author could create - fascination, confusion and loneliness, the heights of ecstasy - as changeable as the sea. Working on a ship puts you inside the novel and you turn with the pages.

I am doing just that. I am aboard the Stella Oceanis; first as casino cashier and shortly afterwards as Social Hostess. I worked with men who were constantly asking me... "Joyce, you okay?" "Joyce, you want something?" "Joyce, you want to have a coffee on the island with me?" Some are genuinely concerned - others want more than coffee.

I am not naive but have learned to be friendly without encouraging romance. I was impressed by one man in particular - the Chief Steward - a Greek Robert Wagner type. A beautiful dresser, in and out of uniform. His professionalism was tempered with kindness, especially towards new crew members. He was an unusual combination of gentle and strong.

Friendships are forged quickly on board a ship. We were all in it and we banded together for strength and sanity. Every second night, a trio met in the ship's tiny library: Patti Parnell, the redheaded English comedienne, the Chief Steward and me. Soon, the boutique manager, Maria, petite and Greek, made it a foursome. The term took on a very different meaning as the scuttlebutt converted friendship into an orgy with the Chief Steward as the sultan. The idea was preposterous but we teased him anyway.

Scuttlebutt is universal among ships and soon the "Foursome" theory was passed along to my Greek boyfriend. I had already told him about our meetings but he sent word saying, "If I catch you doing anything I will kill you." The radio room would receive a call from him. "The Greeks have a saying that it is better to poke your eyes out than to let others speak bad of your name." (I rejected the self-mutilation option.) Then, "Joyce, I got super drunk one night because all the guys were teasing me and I woke up in some girl's bed. A passenger." He was sorry. I considered my fate had I done the same thing. He set the rules of our relationship. In part, they included: You will not say hello to any man, you will complete your duties and go directly to your cabin (no detours), you will not visit ports of call, etc. None of these were acceptable to me. I wondered which one of us was more insane. I consulted my three friends for advice and through them, learned to ignore his ramblings, his phone calls and managed to avoid him when our ships were in port at the same time.

Our foursome kept meeting. It was a small ship, and from our lookout in the library, we watched the late night games. At first, I was shocked. At four A.M., a passenger's cabin door opened and the balding, curly head of an officer moved port to starboard, checking to see that the coast was clear. It wasn't. His face was scarlet as we looked at each other. I knew the passenger and was upset when she told me about her adventure and her plans for the officer's future. She would take him to the States, get him a job and they would live happily ever after. I knew this man would never leave his family. His rationale: "It's all a fantasy. She is here only for the fun and for such a short time. Since I can help make it fun, why not? It's what the women want. I'll be happy to give it."

Because I am on board a Greek ship, I am familiar with their "away from home" philosophy. The Greeks are very conscientious about their families. They are very conscientious about proving their manhood. They manage duplicity so well that it becomes almost reasonable. They have two lives. One at home with their family - the other on board. They are separate and distinct. No problem!

We were a multi national cruise staff and worked well together. As new passengers and new entertainers boarded, trouble boarded with them. One season was particularly memorable when the ship became the largest seagoing bordello west of Suez. The cruise staff was increased greatly so cabins had to be shared by doubling or tripling up.

At embarkation, these were the cabin arrangements:

I shared the cabin with another Social Hostess; two telephone operators shared with a third Social Hostess; the band members doubled up; the flamenco duo had boarded as man and wife (although they weren't) and they shared a cabin; a married singing duo shared; and the comedienne, pianist and male host had separate staterooms.

At disembarkation, these were the cabin arrangements:

The flamenco dancer was seeing the Captain; one hostess was, for a time, sharing the band leader's cabin, then later, the host's; the female singer of the duo was with the saxophonist; the male singer was with a hostess; one telephone operator was substituting for the wife of the Chief Electrician and the other operator was engaged to a steward. I was with the Chief Steward. There was a scramble every 14 days to find substitutes as the cast of characters changed. Although some crew members had a resident girlfriend, this did not discourage them from checking out the passengers. It was the classic three-ring circus with continuous performances. Those women who were spoken for were subject to a relentless pursuit to lure them away from their partners. Failing that, they were gallantly shared. Pity the single female passenger.

An 18-hour day was not unusual for us as Social Hostess and Cruise Director. We were there to load the tour busses and escort the passengers if necessary. We ran the games and the special theme nights. We prepared port lectures. We comforted those who were ill or who lost loved ones. How then, was there time and place for a love affair? Simple management, that's all. After meals or shore excursions, there were hours when the ship was ours. At first, we went ashore to have drinks. At the season's end, we were too exhausted for any activity except lovemaking. We did not enjoy weekends or even days off. We learned to appreciate hours off and made the best of them.

Many women were repeat passengers. They returned each year to renew their longstanding affairs with crew members. Some of the passengers were married and needed to keep "romance" alive; some had low self esteem and there is no therapy more effective than the cruise they booked. For others, it was a rest stop on the rat race of life. I think, from my years of experience, that unless you are very secure in your identity, you can be hurt and perhaps destroyed by playing this dangerous game.

It is also dangerous for the crew. A "woman scorned" can be a disastrous threat. Calls can be put through in the middle of the night, the Line can be contacted with contrived complaints against a crew member or in some cases, a wife can be called. She may not understand English, but does have the universal trait of all wives - she can smell a rat. Many the crew member has been caught when his home number in Greece has been discovered.

Imagine the face of the man who opened the package from his former cabin mate; only to discover an intact grenade with the accompanying message that he would be torn to pieces as her heart was; or the letter containing pubic hair, promising that the next mailing would contain her skin unless, "You leave your wife."

"Seasonal engagements" were much in fashion on board. Some involved people who were already married and ended when the season did. It was common for a married crew member to claim to be separated from his wife, who usually appeared two cruises later - happy to be reunited with her husband.

I was not exempt from this way of life, as I had involved myself with a married man. Also, I was trying to deal with the differences between me and my tyrannical boyfriend. I was growing up faster than I cared to. The blinders of youth were being replaced by peripheral vision.

I had the rare opportunity of working with my boyfriend on the same ship. It was a salvage effort. We had lasted four years. Could we solve our differences? This working arrangement was much frowned upon by both the office and the onboard powers. It required discretion and cooperation from the other officers for protection.

As Social Hostess, I was trusted and relied upon by the Staff Captain. A handsome man - tanned and athletic and a magnet for the women. Unfortunately, five of the ladies whose lives he had enriched on previous cruises were all scheduled for the same ten-day cruise. Mercifully, they did not know each other. I could hardly wait to get to his office to tell him the news. A strategy meeting was held immediately. Other staff would try to divert the attention of the returnees but they wanted only the Staff Captain. He hosted two tables for that cruise. I had placed two of his fans at his table one night and three on another. The married women with husbands were put next to the host, their husbands next to me and the other guests were evenly distributed around the Captain's table. Each of the returning fans was vying for the attention of the host, who was, on the surface, handling himself very well. One of the girls was sitting across the table from him and I soon felt a crawling sensation on my leg. Thinking the Staff Captain was trying to get my attention, I responded by looking directly at him. He was not looking at me. The table guest in question was stretching her leg under the table, her toes moving sensuously up what she assumed was the Captain's leg. It wasn't. Nor was it she who felt his toes under the table. I did! I had the double and dubious pleasure for at least fifteen minutes until the ritual stopped. At the end of the cruise, we composed farewell letters to all the girls he'd loved before and the Staff Captain vowed he would never do it again... ever.

The Electricians' department was represented by a not-that-handsome, but sexually appealing (they said) Greek. He was married, had a girlfriend on board and if a passenger appealed to him, he was in hot pursuit. Both women were oblivious to his actions. The girlfriend proudly told me of his devotion to her. I was quiet, sad and disillusioned.

They knew I could be trusted, these crew members, and every day I listened to stories of their victories. By nighttime, I used to imagine the band playing for musical cabins. When the music stopped, everyone would jump out of bed and go to the next cabin. It was not that far from reality.

My roommate and I were not exempt from voyeurs. We discovered the Chief Purser lying outside our cabin, trying to peer through the vents. How long had he been there? What would our fate be if we reported him? He knew we would be quiet out of fear of his important position. I couldn't sleep, even though it was 2 A.M., so I dressed and went out to the deck. I leaned on the heavily waxed mahogany railing shining bright as a soldier's boot. I watched the sameness of the pattern the ship cut into the calm murky sea. I listened as the splashes of white water rolled away in semicircles from the vessel. Looking down to the faded outlines of a shuffleboard court gave me the sensation of being on the older ocean liners. Tiny puffs of soot left the stack and disappeared into the night air. The vessel was freshly painted with the navy and white logo of the Line. My face was still hot from stress and the sea mist comforted it and blew my strawberry blond hair away from my shoulders. The curl that I painstakingly made every morning was lost to the humid air and I didn't care. I needed to be alone to start classifying my emotions and storing them for a time I knew they would be needed.

Suddenly there was the sound of a woman whining. She must need help but where was she? The sound was coming from the lifeboat directly above my head. I stood on tiptoe, pulled myself up to the edge of the lifeboat and Voila! Two naked women and a waiter had formed the classic ménage a trois. This was too much. I ran to my cabin in tears, asking God as I rushed through the companionways to please slow things down and while He was at it, to please not allow any more Peeping Toms outside the cabin. I fell asleep immediately.

The next day I started mentally listing places for onboard "engagements". They are, in part: Behind: chairs and couches, curtains, show costumes and bars. Under: counters, deck chairs and Inside: the ship's funnel, the engine room or above the bridge under the stars. In: the volleyball court, the sauna, the Jacuzzi, the galley, the pantry and the linen closets. Not to mention the hospital bed or examining room. The nightly practice of draining the pool provided ample space to the couples who could handle the ladders. Romance was everywhere and not to be denied.

There are those who leave a spoor of sadism, having been put on earth to cause pain. One perfect example was the animal-like Chief Purser. He terrorized the local Greek girls brought on board as port lecturers. The entire crew suffered from his rages. If any of the female cruise staff had boyfriends, we paid heavily for that. A dear close friend of mine was a prime target for his tirades. She had a steady boyfriend for seven years and he was not in a position to save her from the Chief Purser. Her gentility and intelligence and fluency in six languages did nothing but annoy him. The boor went to the shipping office and roared loudly enough for three decks to hear him as well as her father, who worked there. He proclaimed her a participant in nightly orgies, a heavy drinker and generally unpopular. This time his ranting fell on deaf ears as the office knew better and refused to discharge this woman. This escalated his temper tantrums. He pounded walls, tables and chairs with his fists. He used foul language and didn't spare the passengers from it. He prowled through the ship searching for something and someone to attack.

After we caught him trying to spy on us through the vents in our cabin door, he was not actively after me. He did tell me that he was going on vacation that very day but I would surely see him again. He left and we could all breathe easily again. We heard that ten men had been fired from the company for embezzlement. Was he one of them? If only he would be. We celebrated at the open crew bar. I could not stop shaking and told my friend, Amalia, I had a terrible fear that the Chief Purser and I would meet again. I knew it wasn't over. Amalia hugged me to comfort me but I was still scared.

During the next six years, I worked on all three ships of the Line. The Stella Solaris, the Stella Oceanis and the Stella Maris. The crew was one nationality - Greek- their customs, their beliefs and their mentality was the same and in spite of the usual arguments, they presented one face to the public.

My boyfriend and I went to Greece for a vacation after an eight-month contract on the Stella Solaris. I had told one of the hosts he could stay the night with us while his girlfriend explained him to her parents. My boyfriend went totally insane at the idea of a male house-guest. As the poor man ran to escape, I was being strangled. I kicked out at him but it was useless. I tried to push him away. Useless. I grabbed a chair and beat him over the head with it. A neighbor heard the commotion and came to the door. I ran into her arms in hysterics. This was too much. I packed what I needed, stayed with friends for a week, and asked the office for a transfer to the Stella Oceanis. I got it.

I had ended the relationship but he would not leave me in peace. The Chief Steward knew this and came to my cabin one night to ask if I was okay. I ran to his arms crying and the affair began. The timing was right. We stopped thinking logically or morally and all we knew was each other. We realized later that we actually were in love. Neither of us was willing to hurt his wife or child, so we were together only when we worked the same ship. We had wonderful memories - in Rhodes at Anthony Quinn Beach and then Patmos at six in the morning where the smell of freshly brewed coffee came over the whitewashed wall to us. Patmos, where a pair of man's fingers crept slowly one by one over the wall. Just as a dusty brown head started to appear, I let out a yelp that would frighten a dragon away. We would laugh every time we remembered that. We drank piña coladas in San

Juan that did nothing to cool our passion. We were friends and soul mates and we were SuperGlue bound. We kept our times together discreet and we were always aware of the commitment he had and respectful of it. I cried many nights for the love I felt and the guilt I had over his wife. She was a kind and generous woman. We became friends and enjoyed being with each other. I took care of their beautiful daughter. How could I possibly be plotting to steal this man from his family. Was I that selfish? Yes, I was. I had a fantastic two and a half years with him and didn't know how to leave him. When an offer from another company came and he accepted it, the decision was made for me. Although my heart nearly broke when he left, it would end up to be a turning point in my moral standards. It was a blessing.

A year later, his wife passed away from breast cancer. He was not with her. He was countries away and he was with another woman. This shattered the remaining emotions I held for him into tiny fragments. I was furious with him. I was still guilty. She was gone and now he was gone as well. Suddenly, the saying, "What goes around comes around" applied directly to me. I never will regret what I did and I never will repeat it.

I went back to the Stella Solaris. My ex boyfriend was there and anxious to renew our relationship. I wasn't. I was finding out who I was and I was starting to like what I saw. I wanted to sail to all parts of the earth. Again, the timing was right and two strong wonderful girls, Yvette and Kileen arrived to make us a trio. They gave me the love of God. We shared, as only women can, all our emotions. We forged a friendship that allowed nothing to destroy it and it is as strong today.

Sometimes they can come from nowhere - for no reason. This one had gray hair and thick glasses and was the onboard equivalent of the Chief Purser with two exceptions - she was Italian and she was a known lesbian. She absolutely hated me. I was dating an Italian musician. Was it that that inspired her to hurl a case of Chanel Number 5 at me? Glass shattered throughout the corridor and because it was the perfume, four decks smelled wonderfully French. The crew dining room became a war zone when La Signorina del Chanel was served a glass of milk with an ice cube in it. The hapless waiter had had to carry it six decks below and was trying to keep it cool. She threw glass, milk and ice cube at the wall behind my head. What WAS her problema? Rumors that I was on drugs and was insane came daily. On my boyfriend's birthday, she presented him with a small colorfully wrapped box. A tiny dead bluebird was inside. My boyfriend understood. Death! It was a Mafia symbol. I ignored the harridan. She was tireless. When we went to Italy on vacation, she called every day. She sent a parade of women to tempt him and failing this, she arranged to have someone shoot at us as we were driving. I learned that he was married and never intended to divorce. I was out of there. It was back to the States, to ships, a new company and Joyce taking control of Joyce.

In the following one and a half years, I changed cruise companies twice, had affairs with three men, only to decide, "Who needs them?" A musician in Gloria Estefan's band was too tempting to ignore but once again, he admitted to being married and father of four. I worked, saved money, traveled and enjoyed my own company. I didn't need a man to make me happy. But I knew something was going to happen.

I had no choice in the matter. The military is obligatory in Greece. For the next two years it was boring, uneventful and not of great interest to me, only something I had to do and get it over with. The next two years went rather fast, although at the time, it seemed forever.

I was first stationed near the Corinth Canal for two and a half months of my initial training. They trained us in the use of guns, warfare and equipment bought from the United States and other powerful countries. We entered as soldiers and the direct aim was to turn us into officers ordered by the government; however, I never made it to officer. It took a while for me to find out why they were holding me back. I passed all the tests, I followed all the rules, and my physical health was impeccable. Through careful conversations with my friends and some particular connections, they investigated my problem.

During the war, in fact the day I was born, my father had been arrested for the first time by the German occupation in the 40's because of his resistance. My mother asked for days, "Where is Haris?" He hasn't come to see his son? One day, one of my father's sisters said, "Don't worry Belyio, he has a new job working with the Germans." No one wanted to worry her because she was basically a sweet, fragile and naive woman.

My father had a quiet life. He was a strong-willed character, but enjoyed life for whatever it offered. He owned and ran a small barbershop at the corner of our apartment building. The nearest cafeneo (a small coffee house in Greece) was right next door. He enjoyed his ouzo and aperitifs all afternoon with his buddies and compatriots. Sometimes his shenanigans lasted well into the night. My cousins and I tried on several occasions to play pranks on our fathers. As they drank, they would sing at the top of their lungs and just plain enjoyed their lives. One night we pulled and slid down the metal doors over them and left them inside without a way to get out. Fortunately, they laughed and didn't get mad for we left them there a long time.

My father was arrested once again when I was about three years old. This time by the Greek government, putting him in exile for having leftist beliefs. It's not that he fully believed in communism, but he was definitely not right wing. During the Marshall Plan, money was given to countries like Greece to supposedly recover from the war, but the reality was for the people to overthrow the community of communists and leftist believers - to create a stronger right wing along with winning more votes. After the war, the population supported the leftists. When elections were instituted in Greece, they were considered false. Too often, the leftist concepts were blown out of proportion and exaggerated; thus unfortunately causing them to be misunderstood by many - and still misunderstood today.

During the war, people told on their friends and neighbors; a very common story during the time of war. Whether during the German occupation or during the recovery period, the police had their informers. It was reported on what paper you bought and read, what your conversations included and whom you associated with. Many of these informers made false accusations. If there was someone you didn't like, it was easy during those times to get them into trouble. They would never hold a good position or get ahead in their job. It made life miserable for many people who were good at their work.

The Jews were not the only people who grieved during those times. Thousands and thousands of Russians and Italians lost their lives as well as thousands of Greeks, including women and children while the Germans ransacked, slaughtered and raped entire villages throughout the entire

18

country. Like Pearl Harbor and Hiroshima, there are other incidents that will never be forgotten by the sufferers and their families. Much of the world knows nothing about the Greek tribulations or doesn't want to know. War is war and we all pay as a people. One group should not stand out more than another. The numbers should not matter. Just because another nationality loses less, doesn't mean they hurt any less.

My father never spoke strongly of his beliefs to me. He did not want me to suffer as he had for so many years of his short 55-year life. He thought it better that I grow up experiencing my own way of life; allowing me the growth needed to create my own thoughts and beliefs without influences of his anguish. I greatly admired his strength in the robust and energetic way he wanted to find a pleasurable life to exist with after the war. He was never a wealthy man, but his wealth lived in his heart with song, dance and family vigor.

I was finally advised by my friends that I was not going to become an officer because of the private listing they had on my father during the war. It never mattered much to me to become an officer in the military. It was just a living. I did not have any plans for my life at this time. I just wanted to fulfill my obligation and get on with it.

After Corinthos, I was then sent to Sparta for 15 days. Here is where the army gathered supplies; mostly of oil and fuel, transporting them to the various divisions and stations. The barracks we lived in were not considered home. The thin, mashed down mattresses on the cots left much to be desired. The food was disgusting as well. I learned to save up my butter to eat with my bread. I kept the butter in my dresser drawers. Every day I would find tiny tooth marks from mice imprinted along the side of the butter. I would just cut it away, get my bread and survive with this. This is all I could stomach. I guess all of us think of our mother's cooking when we are forced to endure hard times in the military. I continued to convince myself that two years is not a long time.

I was transferred near Thessaloniki in a village called Nea Halkidona for the next nine months. I worked in the office sending fuel to the units around the area. I was able to go home every few days and enjoy my mom's home *cooking. During this time, I didn't suffer anything. Knowing I wouldn't be an officer, I just did as I was told and when I saw family, I made a good time of it.*

The next full year I was stationed in Scaramaga, near Athens. Again, I simply performed office work; going home daily at three in the afternoon and rising at seven in the morning to get back to base. Once a week I did night duty. I filed necessary papers accordingly, but basically, I slept.

My wife asked me if I ever wanted to get into private or classified reports out of interest of what was written. I truthfully never considered it or even cared. There weren't classified reports around to be read and what was there, I didn't bother with. My curiosity in that respect isn't very high. I don't care.

For me, my two years was over and I was out. Time to go back to work and make a living. Most of my friends in the neighborhood all went to work on the ships. Greece being such a small country, it didn't offer much in the way of work during the 60's. We always found work on the ships and could rely on that time of always having a job to put money in the bank.

With years of schooling, many tests and certificates and a lot of hard work, I acquired my Captain's license in 1980. My first cargo ship as Master was the...

Chapter Three
Whoops!

He was a boisterous old codger. Outwardly, he seemed a bully. Within was a sensitive soul. At the evening shows, he enthusiastically Inspected the ship's dancers from stem to stern, paying particular attention to the stern. The carved oak cane that would steady him as he eased his massive frame into a lounge chair would help extricate him from it. It would aid him as he trudged back to the suite he shared with the Mrs.

The Mrs. was blonde, made up in several layers and managed a set of very long and very black false eyelashes of the Tammy Faye variety. Her bust measurements were impressive and the Mr. was well pleased with the numbers. She was unwavering in her sweetness and had a certain visceral charm.

I liked the Mr. from the time he boarded and planned to tame him.
"Good morning, Mr., how are you today?" I flirted.
"Dear, seeing your face lights up my day." He beamed.
"Oh, I saw you watching those pretty girls last night." I pouted.
"Oh, honey, I love being in love with the idea of loving some gorgeous woman. It keeps my old heart a'poundin'." He grinned.
"See. You are an old softie. You like to pretend you're a hard tough character, but my dear friend, you are a sneaky bugger." He simpered. I won.

Something was happening. Mrs. was constantly nudging the Mr. awake. I had watched this nodding and prodding since he boarded. His gait was hesitant, even with the cane.

On the eighth day out, I was told that a problem occurred during the night with a passenger and that the Captain was now in the suite. I knew who it was. My heart was thumping in my ears as I raced up the stairs.

As soon as she saw me, the Mrs. buried her head in my shoulder and I held her. Somehow the smudge mix of mascara and makeup on my blouse made the scene even more poignant. I led her to the couch and with a look, signaled the Captain that I would take over. I turned around and the Mr. was STILL THERE. I stifled a yelp. It was only the second time I had seen

21

someone who died. The doctor and nurse came to prepare his body and I had to get the Mrs. out of the suite. A woman passenger next door offered her cabin. I assured the new widow that while she freshened up, the cabin steward and I would arrange the packing and other details. She nodded but was in shock. It was obvious that she was totally unprepared to be on her own.

I can relive it, even today. Now she is gone and Vassilis, the steward, and I, wait until the medical team completes their work. We have a bad problem. How do we get this massive body out of the cabin? Desperate means - desperate measures! We wrap three sheets around him to roll him to the floor. He is too wide. Now he is wedged between the beds and in front of the long dresser. I ask the doctor how I am to pack suitcases as the body is blocking the closets and dresser. He answers, "You'll have to step over him" and he leaves the cabin.

I am horror-stricken. I take the suitcases out and start packing. Each time I have to straddle his body, I hike my skirt up. There is barely room to open the dresser drawers. I desperately try not to hit the Mr.'s head with them and also not to look down at him. Not Vassilis! He is fascinated and keeps pulling back the sheets to look at the lifeless face.

"Knock it off, Vassili. You're grossing me out."
"Never mind. I'm just looking. He's all bloated and purple-blue..."
"Shut up. I don't want to hear it."
"Come on, Joyce. It's nothing."
"Knock it off, Vassili. I won't tell you again."

I can hear the shower still running in the other cabin and I warn him, "We don't have much time When she is finished, she will come here right away."

He doesn't care and still lifts the sheets whenever he pleases.

I am shaking and overcome with fear. I fantasize that the Mr. Is not really dead. While I am straddling him, he will jump up and say, "It was all a joke." Vassilis' macabre actions are making my nerves brittle and he simply won't stop.

I find $70 thousand in travelers' checks, two American Express cards, $60 thousand in cash and an address book. I put everything into the Mrs.' purse. My brain is running in all directions: the body between the beds, the large amount of money found, the family members to call, the American Embassy (We were in Grenada), getting the widow home, and there is Vassilis, making sport of the tragedy.

I am straddling the body. The dresser drawer is open and I am taking out the last of the contents. Once again, Vassilis lifts the sheets to have a peek. This is too much. I strike at him with the clothing in my hands. Just then, the body jerks wildly, like a rubber band stretching in opposite directions. Instantly, I pee forcefully through my underwear directly onto the belly of the departed. I groan and wonder if dying is not so bad. Vassilis collapses with hysterical laughter. I can't move my legs. I look down. A spreading yellow stain is reaching the size of a tennis ball. I want to faint but even if I could move, I don't want to land on the Mr. I want to scream but don't want to attract attention. I want to cry but don't have time just now. The Mrs. might arrive any second.

I plead with Vassilis, "Stop laughing and call the doctor. I can't move my legs." He is out of control and now the tears are coming and stinging my eyes. Slowly, slowly, he gets to the phone and calls the Captain. The Master of the vessel arrives. He says that he has to see for himself what the steward has told him about in their native Greek. I am still pleading for someone to call the doctor so that the poor widow does not see this spectacle.

The Captain calls the doctor, puts a bathroom towel over the yellow-stained sheet and the doctor arrives. He gives me a shot of a muscle relaxant in each leg - waits a few minutes and gently taps behind each of my knees. Together, the doctor and the Captain pull me off the body.

The doctor picks up the towel to see for himself what has happened and asks me to explain. I try to hold my wits and what is left of my pride together and announce that I can not talk about it now as the Mrs. is at the door. I turn her around and take her down to the office to explain the necessary procedures. We call her son and tell him what needs to be done. Six long hours pass until we arrive in port. We arrange a flight, convert most of the cash to a check and I slit the lining of her handbag, tuck a small amount of cash inside and sew it up. After some lunch and a few shots of brandy, we put the widow into a cab headed for the airport.

Logistics are the next problem. The local coroner is called to remove the corpse. Rigor mortis has set in. After an hour's conference, it is decided that the body must be un-wedged from between the beds, stood up and removed from the cabin. This takes six men to stand the body erect and wiggle it to the companionway. A stretcher is brought to receive the body. The stretcher is too long to fit in the elevator, so the six pallbearers take the stairs. Midway into the journey, the body coasts off the stretcher and arrives at the landing before the bearers. They scoop up the swaddled body, place it back on the stretcher and the six proceed down the next set of stairs to the swinging Plexiglas doors. Only one half is open and not one stretcher-bearer notices. Hundreds of tiny glass shards explode and crumble to the carpeting. Six pairs of eyes - the Captain, Staff Captain, Doctor, Chief Purser, the Cruise Director and mine, meet another six. I turn my hands outward and whisper to the Cruise Director, "Whoops."

Chapter Four
"Once in a Lifetimers"

Reading cruise itineraries usually appeals to a limited audience. Yet, some cruises are "once in a lifetimers" If you sailed with us, you remember. If you didn't sail with us, welcome aboard to...

THE ANTIQUITY CRUISE OF 1985

We begin in Piraeus, Greece on Sun Line's Stella Maris. The On board lecturer is world-renowned Greek archeologist, Professor Manolis Andronikos. He is a living textbook of his country's history - proud, enthusiastic and a true scholar.

The village of Hydra, with its shops and cafés introduces the Greek culture.

Corinth Canal - sailing between and nearly touching the massive dirt walls dug out for ships to avoid the long journey around the Peloponnese. The canal is now more than 100 years old.

Itea - to the heights of the mysterious and mystical Delphi, home of the Oracle.

Nauplia - visiting Mycenae and Epidaurus, the Tomb of Agamemnon; then to the ampitheater, acoustically perfect, where plays are still performed.

Gytheion - to Sparta & Mystra, the "Pompeii of Byzantium"

Heraklion - Knossos, with its famous palace and a glimpse of the Minoan civilization in a well-preserved state.

Santorini - steep cliffs of volcanic rock and at the top, innumerable shops and cafes. The island is unique for its donkey taxis. In my case, the ride itself was unique. Midway, my donkey went into reverse and clopped his way up to the top backward!

Rhodes - visiting Lindos surrounded by medieval walls constructed by the Knights of St.John in the 13th century and where the Apostle himself weighed anchor for his historic voyage to Ephessos. Anthony Quinn's beach is a perfect backdrop for a romantic swim in a country known for romance. Professor Andronikos tells us about the ancient Greek tradition of tossing an apple to a girl as a proposal of marriage; catching it was acceptance. I think more apples were tossed than marriages performed.

Bodrum - here is the 15th century Castle of St. Peter; built by the Knights of Rhodes and constituting the most splendid monument of Frankish architecture.

Kos - to see the Plane Tree, said to be the oldest in Europe, under which Hippocrates studied and taught. We walk the terraces of the Asklepieion Museum. Professor Andronikos takes us inside the section of the museum closed to the general public. There, lining the walls, are row upon row of plaster penises, breasts, hands, feet and other body parts. The professor explains that Kos is where people came seeking to be cured. Those who could not afford to pay for the physician's services would present a plaster cast of the body part he healed. This as a gift of thanks. The vast number of penises suggests that venereal disease was rampant. The collection of plaster breasts on the walls makes the visitor wonder if cancer ravaged women then as now. Human tribulations always accompany time and we can only hope that knowledge will end the tyranny of disease.

Kusadasi - we visit Ephessos - One of the "Seven Wonders of the Ancient World" Each of the 15 times I have been there I am equally awed at this extraordinary site housing the Temple of Diana. The communal baths with superb water fountains and marble toilets are here; the mosaic sidewalks, and the private homes with built in swimming pools. The Great Theater, seating 25,000 people, is still in use. Here also, are the Thermal Baths of Scolastika - heated by steam circulating under the marble pavement and in the walls. I stood at The Arcadian Way - eyes closed, imagining Mark Antony and Cleopatra riding past me in procession. Etched in the sidewalk is the likeness of a woman, money in hand, and an arrow pointing across the street. I am always amused at the timelessness of a brothel.

Professor Andronikos tells us that only one third of the city has been excavated. What discoveries are buried still! A six by six-foot hut is said to have housed the Virgin Mary. Once a coastal city, the harbor filled with silt and the city was abandoned. Receding water now places Ephessos over 20 miles from shore.

From the port of Dikili we visit Pergamum & Troy once housing a 200,000 volume library - a gift to Cleopatra from Mark Antony. The site of the "Pillar House" next and then to see a replica of the famous Wooden Horse - the Spartan means of reclaiming the beautiful Helen.

We are on the Bosphorus - sailing between continents - Asia and Europe. What a sight! We touch European soil now, at...

Istanbul - once Constantinople, to tour the Roman Hippodrome, the Blue Mosque, the splendors of the Ottoman Empire, and the historic church of Aghia Sofia. We visit the Topkapi Museum, once home to the Sultans and their harems (the women's ages ranged from 60 to twelve years). Here the largest emerald in the world is on exhibit. Priceless gems; rubies, diamonds, and sapphires were embedded into crowns of gold and silver, chairs, jewelry boxes, walls, silverware, and trays: all here! I mourned loudly for what I would never have, and we continued to the Mosque of Suleiman the Magnificent- eerie and dank. Then to the exotic Grand Bazaar with 4,000 tiny shops offering every item imaginable for sale. Each store was once a stall for one of the Sultan's horses.

We view Mount Athos, with its monasteries and hermitages, from the ship. A law of 1050 restricts women from visiting, stating, "Our Lady to be the last woman to visit the Holy Mountain". Therefore, only men with a Visa marked 'Diamonitirio' are allowed there. These monasteries are full of priceless art, libraries, mosaics, relics and icons. One man showed us a Polaroid of several hundred skulls, thrown carelessly on top of each other in a basement of the monastery. These were all that remained of the monks and priests who once lived and worked there. "Thank you very much, I'm glad I remained on the ship".

From Volos we visit Meteora Pileon where monasteries holding Frescoes of Bible scenes are nestled between giant pillars of mountains rising 600 meters above sea level. Most important is the Church of the

Transfiguration, built in 1545 with its delicate twelve-sided dome and a library with manuscripts and rare books.

We visit Syros and Ano Syros, a traditional settlement built on the rocks from the 13th century.

At Delos we see the Apollo Sanctuary, the Terrace of the Lions (now in the Athens museum) the House of the Trident and the home of Cleopatra and Dyonisos.

Mykonos - the tourists' Mecca for shopping and atmosphere. The last tender was about to leave for the ship's evening sailing. I raced through the brightly lighted narrow rock-covered pavement of a village that is a maze of white-washed, perfectly kept houses. I finally found the harbor when I was suddenly yanked off my feet by a bruising grip on my shoulders. Next to me, beet-red, was a well-built elderly fisherman. "Prox-so-he," he gruffly said. "Uh," I replied. "Be-car-full. Look, pel-i-kan read-y to ate you." I whirled around to find at eye level, an extremely large pelican beak poised to chomp down on a human dinner. I nearly fainted. I thanked the man, asked him to move the bird and boarded the tender with 30 seconds to spare. My heartbeat was louder than the sound of the chugging motor.

Paros - the Byzantine Church, the old castle and ending it all with a typical Greek meal - mouth watering meatballs, feta cheese, dolmades (grape leaves), fresh octopus and an unlimited supply of ouzo. Euphoria best described our mood as we reboarded the ship.

Just as some itineraries are "once in a lifetimers", so was our beloved Professor Andronikos, who graced us every moment with his charm, expertise, limitless knowledge and his amazing wit. He treated every one with respect and courtesy. I sensed he was close to tears when he once dropped 200 slides five minutes before his presentation. I persuaded him to go on and promised I would have them ready and I did. Professor Andronikos is the discoverer of Philippos's tomb, (the father of Alexander the Great). He shared with us some of the last 'gold' artifacts, which are now on display in the Athens Museum. Asked what his emotions were at his historic discovery he replied, "The awesome feeling finding this tomb after thousands of years was a shockingly silent moment." With moistened cheeks, trembling hands and in a compelling Greek accent he continued,

"The Greek language is famous for its sense and ability to portray tragedy, love and emotion easily. But at that moment I realized I had finally found this tomb, not one uttered sound would pass my lips. The love of my country's history just paid me back of all those back breaking patient years of searching to restore the history for all of us to learn. I will one day find Alexander the Great."

I returned to Greece in 1992 planning to visit the Professor. I was heartbroken to learn that in his prime he had passed away due to a heart attack. He, as well as his contributions to history, is irreplaceable.

I recognized that I was physically in places of immense historic importance. I realized I was in the presence of an historian who was so proud of his heritage that he spent his entire short life searching for relics of that history. He was determined to find the burial site of Alexander the Great. How I wish he had been able to do this. Only now, 15 years later, do I truly appreciate the historic significance of what I saw and experienced. Perhaps it is true that youth is wasted on the young.

CHAPTER-IV-B
Mediterranean Cruises

For the Mediterranean cruises I worked on Sun Line's Stella Maris, Stella Oceanis and the Stella Solaris; sailing from and returning to the port of Piraeus, Greece for

Dikili, Istanbul, Kusadasi - Turkey
Alexandria and Port Said - Egypt
Ashdod - Israel
Rhodes, Heraklion, Santorini, Delos, Mykonos and Samos - Greece

These cruises were offered in various lengths, so for a short holiday, several of us went to tour Cairo; to return in three days to the ship at Port Said. From our hotel we watched the dramatic sound and light show at the Pyramids. Then we walked along brightly-lit shops lining the dusty roadway. Suddenly, I was grabbed by my shoulders and yanked into a room. I was blinded by an intense blue-white light. My eyes adjusted to make out two grizzly dark bearded hairy men looming over me. A long white sheet-type dress covered their massive dumpy figures. Flashing black eyes were set off by their artistically wound gray turbans. "Buy something", they gruffly insisted. "Let me go.", I shouted and started for the door. The door was kicked closed. Now I was furious. I screamed so loudly I scared myself. The door was flung open, wedging me between the wall and the door. A sickening thump and the throbbing in my head began. I was roughly pushed outside by a handsome olive-skinned man who arrived in a white uniform set off by an orange vest. He was holding a gun with a knife-like object attached. My stunned friends were waiting. "Let's just go, I have a headache." I said.

The next day, we went to Giza for a camel ride to the Pyramids lined up like Baby, Mama and Papa bears. Isolated in the surrounding sand, these architectural wonders seem almost out of place. A guide hoisted me up on a drooling squatting camel. Each beast was to be led on a designated route by a guide. Not my camel. Wrenching the reins out of his master's hand he galloped off in the opposite direction. He had his own route in mind. I heard screaming and realized that one of my friends was aboard a camel which was in hot pursuit. For those who have ridden a camel, it is easy to recall that helpless feeling as you are jostled in every direction. I was sure I would fall off if I turned around and my head still ached. Twenty minutes later, the camels suddenly dropped down, folding their long legs under them. Even so, it was impossible to get down from that height, wedged, as we were, between their humps. Suddenly, there were camel masters grabbing the reins and swatting the legs of the beasts to urge them up. We begged to get off but no one listened. When we at last got to level ground, we all agreed. No more camel rides, ever. When I finally entered the Pyramid I had a sense of excitement mixed with claustrophobia. I was realistic enough to know the treasures were long since gone to robbers, but...

At the Cairo museum I was impressed and somewhat intimidated by the massive statues. I asked a guard what was behind a particular gate. "Why, go see for yourself." he motioned, "Good, I think I'll do that, thank you very much." Here was King Tut's mummy laid out in a glass case; gold and jewels surrounding him. Here was the boy king who married and died still almost a child. He was small boned but powerfully built and in perfect proportion. King Tutankhamen's olive eyes were oval shaped and his nose

30

small and distinguished. The chin was square and prominent and the lips were inviting. God made perfection in this one human but certainly did not allow him long on earth. Centuries later, this mummy still commands respect. The artifacts left with him to ensure comfort on his journey were priceless. Here, in the Cairo museum, is timeless unsurpassed splendor. At the papyrus factory I bought samples to remind me of a time when papyrus was the common writing material.

The old city of Cairo is surrounded by a great wall where the poorest of the poor dig holes for shelter. Horses's heads are thrown into the streets as food to be fought over, yet there is tremendous wealth here I could not emotionally cope with what I was seeing - Children caked in dirt, wearing clothes so tattered that it seemed useless to wear them; relieving themselves on the streets, never knowing what a toilet is. Each time I saw another urchin with a toothless smile and begging eyes, waves of sorrow surged through me. I prayed for God's help.

We toured Jerusalem, Bethlehem and Tel Aviv where bible history came alive. In Bethlehem, Jesus' birthplace, it was mildly disillusioning to be shown a tiny niche in the corner of a church; yet awe inspiring to think He walked these grounds. We went to the church built over the crypt said to have held Jesus' remains. After a long wait, we ducked into a small door to see a picture of Jesus, some flowers and a square concrete box. We visited the wailing or Western wall - wrote our prayers on a piece of paper and stuffed it into the cracks of the wall (today men and women are segregated there). We walked the narrow shopping streets between the Jewish and Muslim sections. We stopped along a winding road to take pictures. There, two men and a young boy urged us to sit on their camel and donkey. Five dollars would be the price. We gave them the money with the proviso that we would only pose, not ride. But before I could escape, the camel was on his long legs and I was looking down a steep cliff from his back. After enjoying our terror, a sadistic young man had five dollars and a good story to tell. I thought it would be safe in the cab we hailed but just as I was relaxing, someone grabbed my long blond hair through the open window. I screamed in fright and pain. The taxi driver leaned over the front seat and rolled up my window to break the man's grip. We could hear his curses as we drove off. I asked the driver what I did to provoke this and he answered, "You're blond and American. They think you have lots of money and want some of it." All the money I had left was three dollars.

We stopped at the Parliament building and while we were looking at the large Menorah, a large blast shook the ground. "Earthquake?" Then we realized it was a bomb. We raced to a taxi, bypassed the doors and dove through the windows. The driver was roaring with laughter. When we could breathe again, we asked what was so funny. He said, "Why you run, hah hah hah; that is only test bombs from military base. The securest base in the world." "Oh, I see, now I feel real safe. Can we go back to the ship now?" I asked.

When in Kusadasi it seemed only right to patronize the local Turkish bath (hummam). Some of the ship's band members were regulars there and I went with them. It was quiet. The rooms were all concrete. We were led to a large room with tented-off sections where we disrobed and wrapped ourselves in large fluffy white towels. We went to the shower rooms, where only a single detached wall divided girls from the boys. We lay on top of marble slabs. A hairy burly ape-like attendant, carrying a large hard sponge, squirted scented oil on me; then started scrubbing with all his might. OUCH! ECK! UH! This man peeled my skin OFF. I was literally red as a cooked lobster and every pore was on fire. The regulars were quite used to this torture and were laughing at my groans of pain. Even I began laughing just from the lunacy of the whole scene. Suddenly my tormentor was gone. Out from the walls came a spray of water; throwing us off the marble slabs with its force. We couldn't stand up because of the fire hose strength of the water and even if we had succeeded, the oil blanketing our bodies would have prevented it. Even without the aid of mirrors, we knew how funny we must have looked. Minutes later, the water was turned off and another burly man arrived with fresh fluffy towels. We were guided back to our cubbyholes and told to lie on a cot. A new face came in with some warm sweet-smelling oil and massaged it deeply into my still-smarting skin. A fresh pot of sage tea with honey and mint was presented. Then I was told to sleep. This came easily and quickly. When I awakened, a well-dressed Turkish man brought more tea. I paid my ten dollars, said I was happy and left. Yes, the experience was minus the usual amenities, but the raw rugged experience was a treat and my pink baby-skin was absolutely aglow.

CHAPTER IV-C
Halley's Comet Cruises-1985 to 1986

We sail on the Stella Oceanis from San Juan, Puerto Rico, with a cargo of noted astronomers and scientists who trace for us, as we sail, he history of the comet.

The earliest recorded sighting is in 240 B.C. by Chinese astronomers.

We dock at St. Maarten, N.A.- Dutch and French cultures coexist here and aquamarine waters entice visitors.

87 B.C. Julius Caesar was inspired in his conquests by the sight of the comet.

At the port of Martinique, F.W.I. the French influence is evident, both in language and goods.

66 A.D. The comet was observed in Jerusalem by the historian Josephus, who described "a star that resembleth a sword."

We arrive in Soufriere, St. Lucia, W.I. - Here the sulphur smell of the volcanic mountains is said to clear your air passages for healthier breathing.

218 A "fearful flaming star" described by Dion Cassius, prior to Emperor Macrinus death.

451 The comet is rumored to have predicted the defeat of Attila, the Hun.

Castries, St. Lucia, W.I.- The bustling resort city where the film, "Doctor Dolittle" was shot.

530 Black Plague is blamed on the comet's appearance.
Barbados, W.I.- Once the home of the movie star, Claudette Colbert - British influence and magnificent beaches.

684 Violent storms with lightning and thunder with months of unrelenting rain and animal deaths are attributed to the comet.

Tobago, W.I.- Sampling the local rum after a swim in blue-green waters; then a glimpse of Robinson Crusoe's cave.

1066 The Norman conquest of England by King Harold. His defeat by William the Conqueror and his death during the Battle of Hastings was attributed to the comet.

Sailing the "Superb Orinoco" River - Curious Indian children, peeking at us through green and yellow foliage.

1222 Genghis Khan interprets the appearance of the comet as a mandate for him to conquer the world.

Ciudad Guayana, Venezuela - Our first excursion off the ship to view the famous heavenly body. It has long been considered a portent of disaster, affecting both nature and humans; yet it has a serenity about it. Its compelling attraction lies in its mystery.

We boarded busses taking us to a spot miles away from the lights of civilization. We unpacked tripods, boxes of film, food and drink. We skygazers lay on blankets and looked up at a clear starry sky. A cluster forming the comet's tail was directly above us, glittering a welcome. There were expert stargazers with us: Astronomers, Dr. Mark Chartrand, Executive Director of the National Space Institute, Dr. John Eddy, solar astronomer and senior scientist of the High Altitude Observatory in Boulder, Colorado,and Dr. Donald Campbell, Director of the National Astronomy Center Arecibo Observatory in Puerto Rico. They provided a celestial map correct for what we would be viewing. Astonishingly, we saw both the comet and the Northern Lights. It looked as if the sea was in reverse position over our heads. This happens only when the skies are perfectly clear all the way to the North Pole and the reflection of the northern sky can be seen in the southern latitudes. This is a mystical marriage of sea and sky. I saw these lights once before in the 1970's in Wisconsin. My father awakened us at 2:30 A.M. to go outside, lie on the grass and watch the same phenomenon that now thrills me again.

1301 The artist Giotto di Bondone was inspired to paint in the comet in his "Adoration of the Magi". The European Space Agency's mission to study the comet honors the artist with a space probe named "Giotto".

I returned to the ship at 5:00A.M. exhausted but exhilarated enough to join the passengers on a local tour. The sun peeked over the horizon - a signal for flocks of beautiful flamingos to fly. When we returned to the ship, I found that even the strong coffee couldn't keep me awake. After a short nap I attended a lecture by Dr. Joseph Chamberlain, Director of Chicago's Adler Planetarium and an authority on celestial navigation.

1456 Legend states that Pope Calixtus III ordered prayers to protect the fearful from the evils of the comet.

Angel Falls and Canaima - We are helicoptered to the top of heaven; 3,000 feet up, to the highest waterfall in the world. It is a place of untouched beauty and you become determined to guard its secrecy. We swam in the jungle-surrounded lakes. The water, although it looked muddy, was not. Its brick-red color is produced by the compound tretinoin which has a softening effect on the skin. We envy the natives, who live in total simplicity and appreciation of their surroundings.

1531 Apianus, the first western astronomer observed that a comet's tail always pointed away from the sun.

In Ciudad Guayana we paid a seven dollar restaurant bill for: grilled chicken with green pepper sauce, juicy twelve-ounce steaks with local spice sauce, french fries, salad, corn on the cob, a vegetable, three bottles of wine, ice cream, chocolate cake, and spiced coffee. We left the local disco one hour before sailing.

1607 Kepler states that comets travel in straight lines and theorizes the comet will never again be observed on earth.

Bequia, W.I.- Noted for its boat builders - rustic and quiet.

St. Vincent, W.I.- A farmer's paradise with crops of bananas and cotton. Black volcanic sand and colorful foliage.

1758 Sir Edmond Halley disproves previous theories and predicts the return to the sun of the comet every 76 years. Although he was not alive to receive the honor, it was at last named and would forever be, Halley's Comet.

Guadeloupe, F.W.I.- Ooh lah lah! The Caribbean French Riviera with all that conjures up - "sensual" best describes this island's mood.

1835 Mark Twain, born a few days after the comet's appearance, prophesied that he would die upon its return. He died on April 21, 1910, the day Halley's Comet reappeared.[1]

Antigua, W.I. - A beach for every day of the year and the famous Nelson's Dockyard.

St. Thomas, U.S.V.I. - Here, history takes a back seat to stores representing a myriad of countries and passengers return to their ships with countless shopping bags.

1986 The year was the eighth sponsored Sun Line cruise expedition marking the reappearance of the legendary comet. It was, to date, the largest and most intense organized scientific effort to present the phenomenon to the public.

2061 The next scheduled arrival date of Halley's Comet. Will I see it at age 102?

Three cruises of varying lengths completed the Halley's Comet adventure: South America, Grand Transatlantic and Four Continents. For the South America leg we sailed from San Juan, St. Thomas, Martinique and a favorite of mine:

Grenada. I am off to Grand Anse Beach where there is a 70 year old, bronzed, bean-pole skinny local I want to see again. He strums a ukulele and when he sings, two shiny white teeth gleam in his wide-lipped mouth. His flowery orange and yellow outfit completes a portrait of a perfectly content free spirit. His music is his gift and you can accept it or not.

Trinidad, W.I.- We see a street fair of the local Rastas (Rastafarians) with singing, colorful costumes; walking "cool" with permanently fixed smiles. Look up and you will see a Rasta atop a light pole smiling down on the street below. Are they smoking the local plant life?

Paramaribo, Surinam - My girlfriend and I took pictures of the Governor's house. Because this was illegal (we didn't know) we were arrested and put in the local version of a paddy wagon. We were delivered to a tiny room with yellow lights and orange-painted walls peeling from humidity and neglect. No one spoke English and we waited in dreadful anticipation. Filth was everywhere and threatening looking characters circled around us. Both of us are blond and obviously not locals. A miniature version of Tom Selleck arrived, mumbling in French, which my friend understood. We had broken the law, we were told. We apologized, explaining that we worked on a ship and only wanted souvenir photographs. Monsieur took the film out of our cameras and told us to leave. We did, and quickly. As soon as we got to the ship we downed two whiskeys and reassured ourselves that we were free citizens. We imagined the Gendarmes laughing over a bottle of wine at their arrest.

Devil's Island - This place is chilling even on a hot day. Stories of these prisoners tortured, left in the blackness of underground cells to rot; many to die from lack of food, defy belief. Yet it was so. Trying to escape was a dinner invitation to the hundreds of waiting sharks that circled the waters. Steve Mc Queen publicized the island with the movie "Papillon". You can still sense the screams of pain in the quiet. I saw a cell where a prisoner had been chained to a wall for nine weeks - where he could only urinate on himself; and where bread and water were force fed to him. I was suddenly cold and trembling. The island was surrounded by natural beauty but inside, the prison was the epitome of ugliness. God's gift to earth used badly by man.

Belem, Brazil - Want crocodile teeth or voodoo charms?·Stop here at the mouth of the Amazon River. Things are much the same as they have been for centuries.

We were at sea for five days; Comet watching, listening to lectures and enjoying pampering the passengers when the announcement came that the United States had bombed Libya. The passengers were excited and asked if they would see anything; were we close to Libya? No, we were several thousand miles away. The Americans were proud of President Reagan and pleased at the prospect of our boys "kicking some butt." I had mixed emotions.

Cabo Sao Vicente in the Cape Verde Islands. A slice of lunar rock just off of North Africa. Under Portuguese rule and influence, it is best described as an artist's colony.

Santa Cruz de Tenerife, Spain - Caribbean Island of Europe. A constant temperature of 72 degrees invites year round visitors. Banana, sugarcane and tobacco fields are cultivated here.

Casablanca, Morocco - The Casbah - the movie star; Betty Hutton, Hemingway, and "Bogie".

Tangier, Morocco - in the morning and the afternoon in... Gibraltar, British Crown Colony, "The Rock". Home of the Barbary Apes; vicious biting thieves secure in their protection under British law. I enjoyed no such protection from their darting attacks to my knees, my hair and my favorite shirt as I tried to wrestle my handbag from their grasp. Sailing out of Gibraltar, we did see several warships passing. Their purpose at sea and ours are in sharp contrast.

Malaga, Spain, is a clean, noisy city and home to many a British expatriate. The Alcazar, built by the Moorish kings, remains as an architectural wonder.

Palma de Mallorca, Spain. Here the beaches, mountains and the city all held beauty just waiting for us. Classical music was playing, complementing the decor of a restaurant that was unforgettable. Its moon-shaped bar, the round stairwell and the elegant restroom with a water fountain seduced us until sunrise.

CHAPTER IV-D
Theater At Sea - 1987

This cruise is one of those "once in an lifetimers" on the Stella Solaris. It was "Applause, Applause" as members of the Theater Guild appeared in scenes from movies, television and Broadway. They appear here in alphabetical order: Colleen Dewhurst, Suellen Estey, Anita Gillette, Ronny Graham, Larry Kert, Tony LoBianco, Max Morath, Patricia Neal, Milo O'Shea and Kitty Sullivan. Also aboard was Brendan Gill, then the drama critic of the New Yorker. He talked on his profession, his standards for critiquing an actor and the work itself. Some actors shared personal and intimate glimpses of their lives; the late Colleen Dewhurst and Patricia

Neal, in particular. Her autobiography, "My Life" includes the story of her strokes, affecting her profession as an actor. She spoke about "The other woman" who was, in this case, her best friend. Her concerns for her children were universal to all mothers.

Colleen Dewhurst, of the unforgettable voice who used it for roles she alone could handle, gave me special evenings and talked about the world and what is in it.

CHAPTER IV-E
Mayan Equinox 1988

The Stella Solaris is on a ten-day voyage in March. We hope to view "The Equinox Serpent Descending" at the Mayan ruins of Chichen Itza. It will be, as always, a breathtaking and humbling sight. We sail from Ft. Lauderdale, Florida to Santos Tomas de Castilla, Guatelmala - We enter into a demi-jungle. Our driver puts us on a deserted dusty red road for miles, past thatched houses and children playing with goats. He stops suddenly, pointing out a path for us to follow. We range between confusion and anxiety but we follow the path. To our delight, we are facing an enclave with encircling vines overlooking a 40-foot waterfall. A small red dirt beach borders it. We undress, climb the falls and dive into what feels like a liquid iceberg. For hours, we enjoyed the sandwiches and wine we packed.

Isla de Roatan, Honduras - A place of exquisite intense beauty - unpolluted, undeveloped with tropical rainforests and the world's second largest barrier reef. We snorkel at Coxen Hole where the marine life is spectacular.

Playa del Carmen, Mexico - A four hour bus ride, and we are barely able to peel our skin off the blue vinyl seats as we arrive in the hot-house heat of Chichen-Itza; the most visited and important example of the Mayan archaeological temples. There are others at Tulum, Ixmal, and Coba. The ceremonial areas, the Pyramids, temples, monuments and vast courtyards are testaments of the Mayan architecture, art and astronomy. It is March 21, the Vernal equinox and we have clear skies, so that the "Serpent" can be seen. Speakers in archaeology, anthropology, astronomy and archaeoastronomy lecture on their fields of expertise. Settling down on the yellowish grass we watched the sun move across the sky casting a shadow on the northeast corner of the El Castillo pyramid. On the west side of the balustrades, rippling triangular shadows form the "serpent's" long wavy body. When the sun peaked at 4:00P.M. the wide mouth of the "serpent" opened at the bottom step. Hundreds of camera shutters clicked "as the mysterious creature dared to show his features, no one ventured near the shadow, the serpent needed his space". The phenomenon, occurring at the Vernal and Autumnal equinoxes, remains a mystery to students of the Mayan culture. Its fascination is unrelenting. The Pyramid itself is described:

"This structure has four stairways looking to the four directions of the world... with 91 steps to each that are killing to climb." "Modern reconstruction verifies that each of the four stairways has 91 steps. Together they add up to 364, and the top platform-the last step shared by all four staircases-makes 365. This is the number of days in the year. We should not attribute its appearance here to the luck of the draw. There is numerological symbolism in other Mesoamerican pyramids as well."[2]

Cozumel, Mexico - Mexican wares, beaches for snorkeling, and many restaurants.

Grand Cayman, Cayman Islands - Here the turtle rules, you can swim with stingrays and become addicted to the resident rum cake.

And we dock at Fort Lauderdale, Florida.

CHAPTER IV-F
47-55 Day Circumnavigation Around South America

The Britanis, Greek Registry, operated this long cruise from Miami, Florida, Cozumel, Mexico, Cristobal, Panama to the Gatun Lock through the Panama Canal - The engineering technology required to fill the locks; to raise and lower ships to equal the level of the canal never fails to be impressive. For us, it is eight minutes for the lock to be filled with thousands of gallons of water and we are raised up and can pass through the canal from Atlantic to Pacific. It is a feat that requires concerted action from both humans and machinery.

King Neptune holds court as we cross the equator. The astronomer opens the ceremonies with a spiritual dance. He introduces the honorary king's mother (usually the oldest female passenger) He and his Queen are presented with gifts by the Shellbacks and Pollywogs, who enjoy the royal protection from banishment to the depths below. The Queen, unmoved, is disapproving of all the gifts. Thus, the Pollywogs are anointed by the dreaded guard with a mixture of cooked noodles, thick gooey pink sauce, broken eggs, salami and raw fish. The unfortunate creatures are then roughly pushed into a pool darkened from all the food residue. I presented a very personal gift to the King. I artistically painted my bare (nearly) body to match the pastel pink and blue blanket covering me. Kneeling before his Majesty, I opened the blanket and offered my service to him. A collective gasp of shock ran throughout the court. It was more illusion than reality as no one saw the bathing suit bottom I had camouflaged. The Queen was "not amused" and I was dunked in a pool of water, black from foods and crepe paper. As I climbed out of the pool, I felt something in my bathing suit bottom. I pulled out a large slimy fish; screamed, and tossed it where it landed on an 84 year old passenger who became hysterical.

Pizza, Bloody Marys and champagne are served to all for a giddy morning of fun. Everyone receives a traditional authentic certificate for valor and humor for crossing the Equator as a seafaring survivor.

The Galapagos Islands - The government of Equador grants limited travel permits to ensure the safety and preservation of the natural reserves of coral, fish and animal life here.

Callao, Peru - We flew over Nazca to view unexplained formations of naturally drawn geometrical figures dating to the pre-Inca era. The surrounding land was barren, except for them. Over Cuzco we were at 13,000 feet. There was oxygen available for those who might have difficulty breathing. Immediately, we were given tea made from the coca plant; the same one that produces cocaine although the tea leaf does not have the same strength. This plant allows oxygen to flow throughout the body to counteract the lightheadedness due to oxygen deprivation at high altitudes. Out of our 400 passengers, not one became ill. For two days we toured the local area. We heard lectures about the Quechua Indians and the Spanish and modern influences on their culture.

I was backing up to get a better photograph; never realizing I was about to play bookends with an Alpaca (similar to a llama). We bumped buns. As we turned to look at each other, the beast spit at me with deadly aim. I screeched in shock as a large wad of mucus slipped down my sweater. The ship's photographer caught the moment and I cherish the picture.

We survived a harrowing bus ride on a narrow mountainous road and then we were standing in front of Machu Picchu, with an elevation of 1,300 feet. Here was a city located in an impossibly remote area on top of a mountain surrounded by cliffs. Archeologists are still puzzling over finding the remains of only women and children. Stone steps extended up the entire mountain height on one side; a tourist road was carved on another and a guarded tower, forbidding visitors, was on the other side. The construction of Machu Picchu and the manpower to maintain it remains a mystery.

I touched the sacred stone that Shirley MacLaine made famous during her search for her true identity. I prayed for understanding and knowledge and for the lost souls who once lived here. I then listened to the lectures, questions and conversations of visitors. This perfectly preserved city was carved out of solid rock. The buildings were intact, minus only the thatched roofs. I felt in harmony with all around me as I tried to envision what life once was here. A chill shook me as I tried to conjure up the spirits of those who had stood where I did now.

A tour of Lima ended this tour and we were off to...

Valparaiso, Chile - From here, it was a bus ride to Santiago; a city blanketed by a shocking amount of pollution but with Switzerland like beauty.

Puerto Montt, Chile - The fisherman's wharf, seafood market and on to the vast blue Lake Llanquihue.

The Straits of Magellan - We were lectured by the British anthropologist Nick Saunders, who presented his slides and a lecture that surpassed all textbooks. How Magellan was able to navigate through this cold vast area without the equipment of modern vessels is beyond comprehension.

We pulled a stunt on the passengers. It was announced over the intercom that we were going to rescue a polar bear in distress. Five passengers, two sailors, the Staff Captain and I were lowered into a lifeboat. At water level we became instant ice masses. The splashes of water that hit the sailors were ice picks. I had brought a bottle of whiskey which I passed around for momentary warmth. We rounded an iceberg, disappearing from view of the ship. We returned with a massive stuffed white polar bear. The onboard passengers couldn't tell it wasn't alive until we pulled alongside. The screams of laughter somehow made up for our numb ears.

We were overnight in Punta Arenas, Chile. Here we could enjoy the tranquility of an isolated village where once there had been five native tribes in the area. We were taken to the very 'point' of the continent to Puerto del Hambre (Port Famine). We were viewing the end of a treacherous land and the beginning of a perilous sea. It was awesome.

Tierra Del Fuego, Beagle Channel and sailing around Cape Horn filled three days at sea. The clouds were dark and ominous as always. Once, Indians lit bonfires to guide clipper ships through this area. We are entertained by countless hundreds of penguins constantly sliding off glaciers into the black depths of the channel.

The ship was rolling and pitching as we sailed around Cape Horn. A small mound with a tiny red building atop could be seen through the sea fog. This is the station where guard duty is rotated every six months. The loneliness must have been either a blessing or a torture. In the ship's casino was a woman in a wheelchair, rolling from port to starboard and back again with the motion of the ship. She was giggling so enthusiastically that her teeth fell out, much to her own amusement. Her wig was next and then her blouse opened. The audience of elderly gentlemen were denied an encore because I rescued her. To my surprise, she was entirely sober.

The following year when we returned, the sky was cloudless, the sun shone on a sea of glass as we spotted steamer ducks flying. Penguins and silver headed geese were mounting flight as we watched in amazement. Here is a perfect blend of sea, land and weather.

We visit Puerto Madryn, Argentina - founded in 1865 by Welsh immigrants and named for Madryn Castle in Wales.

The air was nippy with cold as I left the ship. Strange groaning noises came from across the pier and I went to investigate. Five gigantic sea elephants were basking in the sun near the water's edge. They were yawning, flirting and farting their day away. We watched sea lions chasing each other, whales splashing their tails; secure in their own habitat and free from ours. We were amused by a colony of penguins, in formal black and white outfits, orchestrating their own concert. They frolicked on the beach, mated behind bushes, and promenaded around their village. After the end of March, their reproductive cycle ends and they begin their journey back to sea until the next year. Because we were the invaders, I imagined that we were on display. I wondered what our fate would be if we exchanged identities.

Montevideo, Uruguay - The Monaco of South America. The scuttled German Pocket Battleship "Graf Spee" was kept here providing a reminder of the wide area affected by World War II. This is a monied, sophisticated city catering to those with matching tastes.

Buenos Aires, Argentina - The Paris of South America. A cosmopolitan city with surprising contrasts between the roughness and Show-manship of the famous Gauchos and graceful European sidewalks and outdoor cafes. The Argentine remains the purest form of the tango. The beef was as advertised - delicious. We visit the tomb of Eva Peron. It was not difficult to identify because of the constant flow of admirers leaving flowers. Her elaborate casket can be seen through the tiny glass window of the tomb. The miniature caskets of children upset me greatly. We were just leaving when something drew me to a particular tomb. I glanced back. The sun was shining through the stained glass window onto a statue of the Virgin Mary. On the left side was an infant's casket; on the right, an adult's. Suddenly, a strong gust of wind blew against my legs knocking me off balance. I stepped back to look at the door assuming there was a hole in it, but it was tightly sealed. I ran from the door. Once outside my legs became weak and I could not walk. Something was back there. Who was it 'who' wanted me? What did they want of me? I wasn't afraid of losing my life. I still wonder what would happen had I returned.

A team of the famous gauchos was the highlight of the local entertainment. The synchronized movements, the athleticism and blazing speed of their performance labeled them "once in a lifetimers".

Rio de Janeiro, Brazil - The typical tourist visits: The Hippie Market, takes a cable car ride to the towering sculpture of Christ, then visits the famous beaches to stare at the bikinis and their owners.

A group of us went to a bar I remembered from a previous visit where musicians came after their gigs to play a jam session. There was music and the curtain opened on a donkey, a dog, a horse and various other animals. Several naked men and women appeared on the stage. The rhythm was slow and insistent and sensual. We exchanged sidelong looks and headed, en masse, for the exit. Once on board, we had a long loud laugh but were still having trouble believing what we had almost seen.

There was a collection of women standing at the gate as we pulled away. There was a collection of crew members waving back from the poop deck. Many would end up with venereal disease, and almost all would do it all again.

Salvador, Brazil - Founded by the Portuguese and the capital of Brazil until 1763. The Portuguese influence is strong in the architecture of the churches, the municipal buildings and private homes. African religion is prevalent enough here to support spirit houses for the worshipers.

Recife, Brazil - Located Northeast of Brazil on the Atlantic Coast. The city was grafted along the delta of the Capibaribe river .The beaches and foliage support the reputation of Brazilia as a land of beauty.

Belem, Brazil - the gateway of the Amazon. A visit to the botanical and zoological gardens.

Devil's Island - Learning of two famous residents here: Dreyfus, falsely accused of treason and Henry Charriere (Papillon), who claimed to be the only escapee from the island.

Barbados, B.W.I. - Obviously clean, obviously British ?λ.and a choice of Red Stripe beer or rum punch, or both.

St. Thomas, U.S.V.I.- Where the rum is fine any time of year and more importantly, is cheaper.

Miami, Florida.

You have sailed via the daily programs but I will bet you would be more interested if you had an inside look at life upon the sea.

1. Chronological order of Halley's Comet by Sun Line Cruises Winter 1985/86 cruise brochure written by Ted Pedas.

2. Mayan Equinox quote from "The Equinox Serpent Descends" of the Griffith Observer, September 1982, Vol. 46, No. 9.

Chapter Five
Those in Peril on the Sea (including me)

People want to know what happens on a cruise ship. Whether happy, comical, scary, shocking, distasteful or downright gory, they want to hear it.

These stories are not exaggerated and some are downright gory. Accidents happen; some come with the territory and passengers and crew alike are potential victims.

The older ships had elevator doors of heavy steel. They were uncompromising when they shut and there were times that fingers were caught there and severed. Immediate icing of the part and the ship's surgeon usually produced successful attachment. One passenger, a surgeon, suffered a badly lacerated thumb: every surgeon's nightmare. The ship's doctor repaired the thumb and was later thanked by a healed and grateful colleague. Not all are success stories. Even with caution, accidents happen.

One 20-year veteran crew member awakened with a partially paralyzed sagging face. He habitually slept under the air-conditioning unit with the constant stream of cold air directed on the same side of his face. His therapy was that used for stroke victims and after a year, he was rehabilitated successfully.

We were coming in to Grenada, West Indies. The ropes were tossed out to be hooked around the bollards while the tugboat pushed and the deck hands manually rolled the ropes in tight. An officer was standing on the bow, looking over the railing, making sure we were lining up correctly. As one rope was being adjusted, it snapped without warning. It ricocheted back and sliced the officer's leg just below the knee. He didn't realize what happened until he tried to take a step backward and could not. The look of total non-comprehension in his deep brown eyes is still in my memory. In shock, his skin had taken on an almost transparent look. He was taken to the American Medical Hospital where the bones were set. He was flown to San Juan where a metal plate was inserted for strength. He later flew home to Greece where nine more surgeries were performed. For the rest of his short life he was able to walk without any problems, except for setting off airport security alarms. Sadly, he passed away in his mid-forties from a massive heart attack. If the good die young, Manolis Andriotis was the perfect example. He loved his wife and daughter. He offered friendship and it was returned. Compassion governed his words and actions. His positive outlook was constant and contagious; yet we who loved him, lost him.

In Grenada again, years later, on a different vessel, an Indonesian sailor was standing at the bow when a broken rope wrapped around his body. Reacting like a rubber band, it physically lifted him in the air, then slapped him down hard on the deck. There was instant help for him. The rope was immediately cut away until the place where it was found to be embedded around his brain. Shock and terror took over his mind and body. We prayed for him but were helpless to reverse his fate - life as a cripple.

On still another ship, a young man came on board to work side by side with his father. He was on the poop deck for arrival, standing behind a small oval opening where the ropes were tossed to the waiting boats to attach ashore. The rope was pulled taut. The rope snapped and came straight back into the opening killing the young soul instantly. His father, Pio, remains with the company to this day. He raised his son's two children and encouraged his daughter-in-law to continue her life. I have listened and learned from our treasured talks. Pio's philosophy is; "Life still goes on and those remaining must live it and live it even more."

Compassion and help from passengers is appreciated in a crisis situation. We anchored just offshore on a relatively quiet morning when the weather suddenly turned chaotic. I was standing on the bridge taking videos of the officers trying to get the passengers back to the ship. The tenders were shot straight in the air and brought down with a bang. In one instance the tender just missed the ship and the engineer on the back of the tender fell into the icy waters. He slipped under the ship but came up quickly by grabbing on to the barnacles along the bottom. He tried to distance himself from the tender to avoid being crushed between it and the ship. A life ring was thrown out to him; he grabbed it and was quickly yanked up on the tender by a sailor and a passenger. Two other passengers on the vessel witnessed the incident, ran to the bar, got a bottle of whisky, ran to the gangway and forced him to drink quickly. Our doctor then took over. The patient caught a bad cold but he was safe. He was pampered and cared for by all for the rest of the cruise.

We are vulnerable at sea as on land. We try to be cautious of both our hearts and our physical bodies. Perhaps the confinement of space makes for intensity of reactions. I and my fellow crew are members of a ship-made family - for protection, solace and survival.

I have been there when women learned they were pregnant - some shocked; others pleased. Years ago, a pregnant woman would leave the ship immediately or have an abortion to avoid losing her job. Today, however, the woman is allowed to work with a doctor's permission if the pregnancy happened while on board. The company's insurance will not cover maternity claims in most cases, leaving the patient responsible for payment. Pro-lifers will naturally object to the abortion choice, particularly in the United States. Many other countries encourage it depending on the individual circumstances. It is a financial necessity for many women on board to make money to support family at home. Many pregnancies are carried to term, however, by those who want to substitute sea for land, they use their options. Fewer women working on ships in years past presented fewer problems. Those ships carried 80 to 380 crew members. Out of that number, there were perhaps only five women. Today, the complement is from 600 to 1000 and of these, easily half are women.

The smaller ships produced a very tight community with close friendships. We worked together for a full contract - 11 months. The larger vessels forbid that by their sheer size, and a six-month contract can be over without every crew member meeting.

When AIDS first became publicized, I was ignorant of its scope. My first contact with a victim was a passenger who was wearing a heavy coat, a large scarf, wool pants and thick socks. It was 100 degrees outside. He didn't get off at any port except for Mykonos, Greece. No one wanted to touch him. When he ate, his glass, silverware and plate were thrown away. His sheets, blanket and pillow were thrown away. Rumor was that they were thrown overboard. The passenger was very rough when speaking to the crew and seemed constantly angry. I went to his table and told him to cool it a bit. He told me to "F"-off. I said that was fine. I patted his hand, saying that I could never pretend to understand the frustration and fear he was experiencing but that no one on board was to blame for his plight. I cared, we cared, we just didn't know how. I walked away. He later apologized for his behavior. I told him that "God shall bless you anyway".

Mr. Rock Hudson booked a cruise to the delight of everyone on board. He was a stunningly attractive man. He was rude a few times when told that the rules for passengers applied to him as well; yet even his rudeness had a certain charm. Shortly after he left the ship, it was publicized he had AIDS. We were distressed and bewildered. I felt deeply angry at him for putting others at risk, especially since we had no medical knowledge about the implications of his disease. Now we know, though.

We began losing friends to this disease. Past Captains, Cruise Directors, entertainers, musicians and others, dead from the promiscuous life we lead, for whatever the reasons. Some continue this lifestyle, but the majority takes proper precautions against the spread of the AIDS virus.

Yes, sexually transmitted diseases were and are commonplace among ship's crews, whether from the lack of protection or the excitement of being with someone after months of celibacy. The number of cases is decreasing but still exists.

Death makes its claim wherever it chooses. In past years, an older group was cruising and a weekly death was not unusual. With today's younger clientele, it still happens; it simply happens less often.

My first experience with death was traumatic. I was at dinner and looked across at a man I thought was choking. He was actually suffering a massive heart attack. The ship's surgeon worked him constantly for an hour and lost him. The wife denied any cardiac history on his part. As a widow she then admitted that her husband had suffered two previous heart attacks. I watched a man die within two feet of me. I can relive the entire scenario today. The Chief Steward consoled me with, "Joyce, I know it is sad but it is sad for the remaining family members and loved ones. But for the person, he was happy, he was on a cruise with his wife, enjoying good food, good entertainment and visiting interesting sights. Isn't that the best way to go? Never be sad for the one gone, just pray for the ones remaining."

Those thoughts always help me gain courage even in the sadness of death, whatever the cause.

Suicide happens; fewer times than accidents, but it happens.

My first exposure to suicide involved a strikingly beautiful 16 year-old passenger who boarded with her mother, brother and father. I saw him intentionally stick his foot out and trip the girl. She fell down several stairs and although not physically hurt, was upset. I ran to help her but she refused. She gave the man a piercing look and walked away. That night, I received a call to go to the hospital. In the waiting area were her mother, brother and the man who tripped her. In the treatment room, the nurse and doctor were pumping the girl's stomach. She was drifting in and out of consciousness and asking for me. I held her hand and told her everything would be okay. I asked the mother what had happened. She said she had taken an entire bottle of aspirin and that this was the third attempt. She left and I stayed with the girl. When she was able, she explained that the man was not her father. He was her mother's boyfriend. He frequently appeared in her bedroom at home forcing sexual contact. She could not make her mother understand the situation and she was unable to take the pain any more. I cried. I felt ill and helpless. I was with her as much as possible for the rest of the cruise. When we arrived in Miami, I called the police, told them where this girl lived and what was happening to her. There was no follow up but my prayers are with that beautiful creature.

Suicide can be unexpected. He was a crew member - Greek, young, good looking and a competent worker. His girlfriend, whom he met on board, had left the ship and told him she planned to stay on land. He had been aboard ship for a year waiting for a promised vacation. It never came until the morning when unusual banging sounds were heard coming from his cabin. Then there was a call to his crew mate, next door. Asking would his friend bring him some water. Impossible. The cabin door was locked. The ship's surgeon was called and security opened the door. There was blood everywhere. The doctor worked frantically to insert a balloon-type instrument in his nearly collapsed arteries. The nurse bandaged the wrists that he had severed. He was stabilized. After a hospital stay, he had a rapid recovery and blocked the entire incident from his conscious mind. I don't know what has become of him, but I hope he is safe, healthy and in better spirits.

Early one morning we were notified that a crew member was missing. It was three days before the Millennium New Year. The man had given his wallet to a friend to keep and said that he was leaving. Leaving? The ship was at sea. His friend tried to follow him but lost him. He went to security to inform them of his friend's strange behavior. He disappeared around 3:45 A.M. The officers conducted three separate searches without success. Three hours later, the ship returned to the approximate position where he could have jumped overboard. The passengers were informed of the situation and were asked to help in the search for him or his body. An American Coast Guard helicopter conducted an all-day search and we finally accepted the fact that he was lost at sea.

I felt sick and betrayed. Had no fellow workers seen any signs of odd behavior? I was angry with him, even in death, for his ultimate act of selfishness at age 36. I learned that he was an only child and that only his father would survive him; waking and sleeping with suffering. How could he do this to his father? It was the Millennium New Year cruise - heavily booked and expensive. Most of the passengers were understanding. A few, a very few, had these comments: "Why do we have to go back, it was only a crew member?" "Now look, you all have ruined our vacation, we have lost the port we wanted to see the most." "Why are you crew so thoughtless to the passengers who are paying your salary?" "Couldn't he have done this on his own time?" "Well, you must have a pretty disgusting life here on board if you have to jump to get away from it."

To respond to the first question: we have to return to the alleged scene. Not only because it is International Maritime Law, but for the respect of a human life no matter what the circumstances.

That should be enough gory stories to satisfy anyone. We did have an onboard robbery though, on an evening cruise out of Fort Lauderdale, Florida. After a fun evening, we returned at 3:30 A.M. Two people walked past security at the entrance door to the casino. They put on masks, held up the casino staff and pursers who were counting the money and they walked off the ship. The scuttlebutt started: Security had been tied up - not that I know of. The robbers had toy guns - who knows; they hadn't been fired. They got $100,000 - We had never taken in that much money in one night while I was on board. The money was never retrieved and the robbers were never found.

One night I was running the bets for the wooden Horse racing event. As we were wrapping it up to go, the Orchestra came on stage to start the dancing. I was watching a man with a tan jacket and white shirt dancing wildly with his or someone else's girlfriend or wife. I noticed a deep red spot spreading over the center of his shirt. I pulled him aside and showed him. He looked down, opened his shirt and saw a hole just below his chest. He looked at me. Clunk! He passed out. I called the doctor who attended him instantly. Later, he remembered a fight in the men's room in which he was unexpectedly knocked up against the wall. (The wrong place at the wrong time). He thought he was just elbowed, but indeed it was more dramatic than that. We never found the fighters and no one else was reported hurt.

Sexual harassment; that subject that usually elevates the decibel level in any conversation, does exist on land, on sea and probably in the air. From the time of the first sailing, a ship has been truly a man's world. Women were not treated as equals and were regarded as sex objects. Alexander the Great crossed lands and sailed waters conquering new lands. Probably without much convincing, he encouraged his men to propagate offspring in every village they passed. Alexander's onboard female staff was nonexistent.

Until the 1950's and 60's, modern ships carried only a handful of women. In the early 80's, when I started work, there were only four women and 120 men in crew. It was, quite naturally, open season on us. Handling it becomes an art and a science. When I was approached but unwilling, I said, "I'm flattered, but no thanks." If someone was too insistent, I threatened to go to the Captain, who was the law on the ship. A complaint call to the office would only get me fired. This problem was not even addressed in those years. Later, American girls threatened and even took officers to court. I guess I was not so greedy for a money settlement. The Captain of the ship was always able to stop the harassment without fuss unless he was the guilty party. Then it was handled ever so quietly by the office.

One man however, didn't sexually harass me but permanently damaged my psyche. The culprit was the Chief Purser when I started working on board ships. Ten years later we would meet again on another company. I was petrified to learn he was on board but admit that at first he treated me well. We had some laughs and worked well together. I became the peacemaker among the Greek officers and the English, Canadian and American cruise staff.

When the Chief Purser wanted to begin a relationship, he invited the girl and me, as chaperone, to dinner and it was a very pleasant experience. This all changed within six months when it became official that I was seeing a senior officer. The Chief Purser was an intensely jealous man. If there was a romantic involvement between crew members, he became incensed. He became even wilder if he was rejected by a woman he liked.

I kept my distance from him when I saw the approaching signs of his wrath. I warned the Staff that he was dangerous. They were beyond criticism but that didn't count. He was bent on destroying me.

He bellowed at me in front of passengers. Many of them wanted to report him to the office, but I said no; it only caused more problems. He used filthy language with me in his office with other crew members present. He tried for months to make me surrender to his fury. I never did. I kept my dignity by looking him straight in the eye and not arguing. Yes, I could have gone to the Captain, but they are of the same nationality, so what would I accomplish? I could go to the company, but then that would expose my relationship with a senior officer. Neither of us was married, so that was never a problem. In a "choose one" situation, the woman always ended up packing, so I stayed quiet.

Then one day we had a massive argument, the source of which was a collection of lies his girlfriend had told about me. She was intensely jealous of me for unknown reasons yet admitted to having respect for my professional conduct. I was mystified by the accusations because I was innocent of them.

I was called to his office. He started berating me. I asked him to wait, closed the office door and urged him to continue his speech. He slapped his hand down on his desk calling me a whore, and a conniving disgusting woman. I asked him why the personal name calling when he was supposedly angry with me for a work related problem. He said it didn't matter. I told him that I had had enough and I would report him to the police when we arrived in Miami. I also told him that I had him on tape. That was too much. His face became discolored, his eyes turned a putrid ugly black, his body became distorted, and his anger so escalated I thought he would pop like the weasel. He decompensated. He physically bounced off the walls like a ship in a windstorm. Shaking hysterically, he slammed his fists down on his desk, cracking the glass cover. The complete madness of the scene terrified me. I opened the door to the large crowd that had gathered there. I ran to my boyfriend and told him for the first time about all the previous incidents. I had foolishly thought I could handle the situation alone.

The next day was show and throw. The Chief Purser started calling me names again but this time he directed them to my boyfriend. It is very disrespectful for a Greek to speak badly of another Greek's serious girlfriend or wife. After telling him to shut up (which he wouldn't) my boyfriend struck him, grabbed his throat, threw him against a cabinet and told him to get over it. The report of this traveled at the speed of sound. The Captain called them to his office where they made a truce and guess who was the odd woman out.

I was annoyed when the Chief Purser and my boyfriend seemed to form a friendship. They had drinks together and went ashore together while I was left behind. I was insulted that the Chief Purser got a slap on the wrist instead of a serious reprimand; and worse still, the Captain blamed me for the fight between his officers.

The Chief Purser has never ceased to attack me verbally. He has told his story, painting me as the world's worst to anyone who will listen. I will never totally rid myself of him because he and my husband have mutual friends. To this day, he remains a thorn in my side. I can accept his presence for the sake of my husband, but I NEVER forget. I, as well as many other women, have been abused by him and carry the scars.

Happily, what goes around comes around applies to him. He was eventually fired for falsifying financial statements, a little embezzling and complaints from those who refused to take his abuse; including men. Few cruise Lines will accept him because of his reputation. When this man likes you, it is heaven but if he doesn't, the result is hell with no UP elevator. Fortunately for him, he has a lovely wife and two children. I hope he will learn that people will always rise up against inhumane treatment. Some ask what gives him the right to be happy when he has sacrificed so many in his path. BUT, "Is he truly happy?"

Not only do accidents happen and suicides happen but sometimes the vessel itself has problems. I was on a cruise around South America when we were informed that there was some difficulty with the ship. We were to tell the passengers that a rope became entangled in the rudders. Repairs would be carried out at the next port, thus delaying the following port of call. Frogmen dove under the ship. We had Rear Admirals, Colonels and various other passengers who were ex-military and all were suspicious. Four men approached the Cruise Director and me, telling us to be frank with them. Asked why, they announced that they had watched where the frogmen dove and that the rudders were not nor would ever be located mid ships. We giggled, trying to balance the fact that we were caught in an obvious lie against following the Captain's orders. We confided that there was a small rusted hole at the bottom of the ship. It wasn't a serious concern because the Captain wasn't about to endanger all lives on board. It could wait for repair. We begged them for secrecy.

They didn't tell anyone but they did get even in a subtle way. They convinced the other passengers, the women in particular, to ask the Captain to cut up the offending rope in pieces and give them to the passengers as souvenirs of our delay in port. The Cruise Director and I thought it was terribly funny but the Captain was livid. He shouldn't have expected that story to go unchallenged.

We were sailing out of Barbados when the Captain noticed something on the horizon but off our course. He decided to investigate. The weather was rough with high winds and large waves covered in white caps. He had been right, there was a cargo ship on fire. There had been no SOS, no attempt at communication. Our lifeboats were lowered and sent to collect those trying to scale down the side of the burning ship - 14 Korean crew members. We gave them food and drink and sailed them back to Barbados wrapped in blankets. All hands were accounted for. On our return two weeks later, we found out that a local had heard about the abandoned ship. He rowed himself out in rough weather to claim the vessel. Maritime Law dictates that once the Captain leaves the ship, it is up for grabs. The entrepreneur sold it for scrap for two million dollars.

The Captain speaks:

You can not put a value on life, though many times I would like to for those who cause problems where it isn't needed or wanted.

While traveling on a cruise ship, it is to be for fun; not to hurt. It is to be a vacation, not a tragedy. It is to be exciting, not some personal stimulant for the daring.

One quiet night I was able to go to bed at a decent hour. I was watching TV waiting for my girlfriend, (now my wife), to return to give me a massage. While waiting, I decided to go check on a telephonist whom we had to sedate because of an intense depression she was in. As I walked out the Officer's area, the Chief Radio officer approached me that someone was knocking down our speakers on the outside decks. I picked up the phone to call security when a couple asked for some help. The man explained to me that he was bent down looking closely at a map we had on the wall around the corner when someone threw a pipe (he handed me a curved pipe that looked like it was from a toilet). I asked if he was able to recognize the person if he saw him again and he said yes. I called for security to come take the man around to see if he could find the person. When I put the phone down, a teenage boy walked into the corridor and pulled me along while screaming that someone had pushed many people overboard and needed my help. He was holding me so hard I couldn't get him off. He continued pulling me through the door, but the outside door was solid wood and would cut my arms off if it shut. So I finally pulled hard and got loose. As the door closed, what I saw through the porthole was the boy who turned around, ran and jumped over the railing. I ran out the door, lucky that we were directly behind the bridge, and yelled, "Man overboard turn starboard." The ship turned fast. I thought for sure he was gone under the ship, but I still ran along the ship throwing out several life rings all the while thinking "no way is this dummy alive". We immediately radioed the other ships in proximity, stopped the ship and lowered a lifeboat for search. Forty-five minutes passed and nothing. We were lucky because the Nordic Empress had stopped to help us. One of their crew spotted this guy floating in the water. Our lifeboat had at one time been near him, yet he didn't talk. The other ship took him. I had described what he was wearing to the other Captain to make sure we had the right guy. I thought about what he had told me, that there were other people overboard and that maybe it wasn't him. But it was. We told them to keep him and turn him over to us in the next port. We both were going to Nassau. It goes without saying that we disembarked him sending him back to the states to his family. He was only 18 years old and had a bit too much of everything. He was a very troubled teen who needed help. Though we could have charged him for endangering other passengers, the company didn't want the publicity. My wife disagreed. She gets really angry at those who are trying to sue the company with stupid and false accusations. It was a chance in her mind to have the cruise industry fight back to show we could sue them too for the actions they take.

A comical side of shipboard events is the story of Joyce taking the show off in the Show Lounge. When the ship lurched quickly, she flew across the stage, several chairs wobbled and a couple of passengers still in their chairs, slid a few feet. Joyce didn't know what had happened, of course, but she got composed and told the passengers that, "It seems as though we have crossed the equator tonight early."

The next day 200 passengers came to the information desk asking for maps so that they could mark where and when we crossed this equator. They didn't get it that we were thousands of miles away from it, that we don't bump it when we cross it, or that it isn't located between Miami and Nassau.

I had my one and only fight on board when another senior officer was giving a rude time to my girlfriend, who is now my wife. He wasn't a bad guy. It was just his village ways. I was angry with myself for not taking better control of my mind, however, he turned red accusing her of things she really had not done and wasn't the type of person to do the things he was pinning on her. I lost control when he used vulgar language towards a woman I found myself for the first time becoming very serious with. I lunged at him with great force. I knocked his face into the drawers, grabbed his throat and threatened him to stop. My rage was great. I stumbled back and walked out. I told my girlfriend that she would be hearing stories and not to listen to any of them. Better she didn't know the full story; she was already completely beside herself with his treatment of her. She is the kind, though, that will get your blood boiling, because she doesn't flower her words, she gets directly to the point of -"beware". After we were called to the Captain's office, the officer and I shook hands like children and went out to play.

It was enormously painful for my girlfriend to see me with him all the time; when we two couldn't be seen together publicly. There was no one else for me to converse with. We didn't have a choice of whom we worked with; we had to get along. You either take it or leave it. She isn't a stupid woman; she had to come to terms with this her own way.

Our major concern on board is the fear of fire. Not only will it tragically take human life leaving behind devastation. Not to mention, the ship could sink, costing life, money and jobs. It becomes a tragedy in more ways than we are able to count. A pain, I assure you, I will avoid at all costs.

One day after I went to bed, my girlfriend was coming out of the bathroom telling me she smelled something at the same time that we heard running above our heads. The phone rang and I was informed there was a fire in a crew area down below. I told my girlfriend to stay put and left. There was smoke everywhere and crew running out just in their underclothes. I formed a search team, tied a rope around my waist, took an oxygen tank and crawled my way through the corridor to find the exact location of the fire. It was bad. This was an old ship and the corridors were a maze. The corridors turned one direction, then another, stopped, changed another direction and then another. There seemed no proper end. When I ran out of oxygen, I pulled the rope for the crew to pull me back; I couldn't find the way with all the smoke. I had changed tanks four times. I never put on a fire suit because there was no time. We didn't know the extent of the fire; we had to work fast. In the meantime, they were evacuating passengers from the above cabins to the outside decks. We continued to search what seemed several hours when I finally found it. I tugged the rope for the crew to follow in with the fire equipment. After about two hours we had it out. Seventeen cabins were melted, not only destroyed, actually melted. The sheet metal the ship was built with is the only reason why the ship was saved. It was the best ever made. Today, it seems like paper; not a secure feeling. It is like the way cars were built in the fifties and how thin they are today.

It was haunting to walk the hallways and smell the ashes. The cabin where the fire started actually had the wall adjacent to the corridor ballooned out as if a tremendous ball had been thrown and caught by the wall. The glass cover to the fire extinguisher across the hall was melted down the side of the wall and stuck there. Burnt mattress springs stuck out in every cabin, but there was nothing but these left. All objects, including stereos, TV's, clothes, money, toiletries etc... were completely disintegrated. There was nothing but nothing left. No passenger cabins were destroyed; only the sweat of the smoke along the walls. These people were moved to other cabins. Some of the crew didn't have anything left, just the shorts they had on when they ran from the fire. Some of these men lost their music equipment, money, pictures, everything.

Basically the passengers and rest of the crew were calm. Only a small incident where one staff member mentioned we would probably stop in Cuba for help. We had several Cuban passengers who started to panic. But we were near Cancun, Mexico and at least 16 hours away from Cuba. It was a false rumor and one that was stopped fast.

There was a problem with a schizophrenic nurse from the Philippines who had witnessed a volcano eruption at her home and went wild when the fire started. Joyce had taken her to her cabin she shared with Lynda the Stage Manager. She had torn up their cabin and peed on Lynda's bed. Later she was sedated. We finally got to bed for a couple of hours, then back up to do our daily duties. The fire had been started by a unattended cigarette, which is the cause of the majority of fires. Not only on ships, but everywhere.

We had kind of a crazy few months there.

We had the fire, the boy overboard and while on vacation in Greece, my girlfriend and I were lying on the beach when I looked up and down the beach watching as a pretty blonde was taking all her clothes off. My girlfriend was reading a book, so I didn't disturb her. However, I became concerned when this girl swam farther and farther out not returning. I then tried to point her out to my girlfriend. She then said to call the Coast Guard, maybe she was trying to commit suicide. I walked over to the cabin there on the beach and called. About 40 minutes later they came, asked questions and found her clothes with an Austrian passport that had numerous entry stamps into and out of Greece. It took about 45 minutes to an hour for them to locate her in the water. It was scary because the water was ice cold and she was in the path of the hydrofoils and flying dolphins entering and leaving the harbor to other islands. She could easily have been hit. However, the Coast Guard did retrieve her but she was hypothermic. An ambulance came and took her to the hospital. We didn't go to the hospital to see her for maybe she didn't want to be saved; it was best to let her work out what she needed to.

Two passengers passed away on a cruise from Italy to the Caribbean. A sad event for all, but something that cannot be predicted, managed or understood. One man was already ill, but the other wasn't at all. In fact, he had brought his wife on the cruise because she had survived her battle with cancer. He wanted to treat her to a cruise to help ease the pain she had suffered. Unfortunately, this event changed drastically when he ended up passing away suddenly. Her shock, it goes without saying, was tremendous. Both of these women were asked if they wanted a burial at sea. Both declined for one woman's husband hated the sea and the other was just afraid of it. They felt it wasn't a good resting place for their spouses. Once we got to port and the passengers had disembarked, the bodies were prepared to be taken off. We were at the loading gangway where there was a conveyer belt with rollers that slides supplies and food down from the pier on to the ship. The first body was placed there and rolled up to the pier and taken away. The next one however, started to fall off the belt. The crew helped grab the bag before it fell in the water but it had ripped open showing the body. These poor men screamed and ran away. We then had to get our medical personnel over with a new bag and they finished the project.

I don't have too many experiences where we had accidents other than what has already been written. I did, however, have a time when I was a Captain of a cargo ship where everything seemed to go wrong.

We were on a five and a half month trip that included ports in Sweden, Portugal, Saudi Arabia, Italy, Port of Sudan, Libya and the Suez Canal, all not necessarily in this order. A Danish Corporation had chartered the ship to carry logs of wood, plywood, supplies etc., to these various ports.

We had a situation in which the crew hadn't been paid. The crew contacted the ITF (International Transportation Federation) to report their plight. When they boarded, I informed them that I didn't have the money from the company. ITF gave us five days to get the money. I contacted the company explaining the five-day deadline and we received the funds. We moved on.

Often times, however, it must be mentioned that the crew refused their pay for six or seven months because they would be paid in the currency of the country we were in. So, they would wait until we were in a country where the *rate of that currency was better and demand all that salary due them in that currency. We would not have all the money they were demanding. This resulted in an endless cycle of grief.*

We had really rough seas one night and all the wood stacks that were tied to the outside deck of the ship were washed away. We had a small fire in the smokestack, but were able to control it without hesitation or damage anywhere else on the ship. Later we encountered a lot of fog that slowed our sailing time badly. It is unnerving for a Captain when there is fog for the obvious reason that you can not see anything. I had to remain on the bridge for several hours as we blew the ship's whistle often to warn of our presence to anyone that may be near.

Naturally, we were at sea for several days at a time and even when we were in a harbor, it could take anywhere from two to twenty days to get a berthing to unload and reload due to the traffic at any given port. That is when time grinds on everyone's nerves. Of course, the men wanted to get off and meet some girls to relieve their tension. When they did, a few would sneak the girl to their bunks for as much fulfillment as possible before going out to sea for whatever number of days we would be out again. Really a continuous non-stop cycle. Back then, working on the ship was good money but a very lonely life and made everyone a little animalistic with the close unromantic conditions.

One time we had an extensive wait to get through the Canal. We were running extremely low on water; basically we were running out. We asked the authorities for help. They informed us that we would get water in a couple of hours, then it was the next couple of hours, then it was the next couple of hours. We were using the limited water we had for necessary cooking and drinking, nothing else. For showers we used seawater and basically took several wipe offs. It was three days before we received any water. Again, putting everyone on the edge.

As we sailed in the Suez Canal, the locals came alongside, each with his own dingy. They wanted to buy wood, plywood, paper etc. that we had on board. I informed them we couldn't do that, nothing was for sale. They were hard headed and wouldn't listen; they would climb up the side of the ship and try to get on board. *My men had trouble keeping them away; their insistence was annoying. I finally got my gun and chased them away from the ship. I understand these people's needs, but my obligation is to the company who hired me to get their products from A to B, C and D. We had already lost some of the cargo in the previous storm. I wasn't about to let any more get away.*

The last real problem on this trip was when we arrived in the Port of Sudan where the local authorities arrested the ship. They came on board with papers of the custody, brought the police on board and stayed. The company who had chartered the vessel had gone bankrupt. There was nothing we could do and nowhere to go. After several conversations with the company and a lot more grief, they finally sent the monetary funds needed to pay all of the agents, the authorities and the expenses of the ship. We were then released from custody.

The only really nice thing of nearly half a year was the port of Libya. The crew went out for the first time in a long time enjoying themselves completely. I must say this place was so clean, there was no trouble of any kind. Restaurants, food and entertainment was fantastic and at its best. The local people conducted themselves with dignity, poise and good manners. The shores, the streets, the surroundings were kept well. Fresh. Unpolluted. This put a pleasant lasting impression on me.

Chapter Six
Rule Britanis

I have sailed the currents and ridden the tides on various ships, including: Stella Maris, Stella Oceanis and Stella Solaris with Sun Line Cruises; Discovery I with Discovery Cruises; the Victoria, Amerikanis, Azur, Horizon, Zenith, Meridian, Century, Galaxy and Mercury with Chandris Fantasy and Celebrity Cruises. One ship, however, is special: the Britanis; owned by Chandris Fantasy Cruises. This ship changed the course of my professional and private life. My every emotion intensified and encapsulated itself into the Britanis and we became part of each other.

The ships manufactured in the early 1900's were built to last for tens of years. When they were released from the safety of the yards, they were subject to forces that could harm or destroy them; from running aground to sinking. Only a handful were survivors and the Britanis symbolized them, with a life span that welcomed three generations, transported military personnel, saved lives, and gave pleasure to thousands of multinational crew and passengers alike. The Britanis was a life force - a seagoing Tinkerbelle who brought joy to those who sailed her.

She was born in Quincy, Massachusetts - the last remaining American ship built by Bethlehem Steel. She was christened the S.S. Monterey in October 1931. She first held 472 first class, 229 cabin class and 360 crew cabins. The S.S. Monterey was sister to Lurline and Mariposa. She began her sailing from New York to San Francisco in May 1932 to inaugurate ports of call at Los Angeles, Honolulu, Auckland, Pago Pago, Suva, Sydney and Melbourne. She cut the normal sailing time by one third and created high standards of service to this route.

Those who sailed her early were Barbara Hutton in 1933, Ginger Rogers in 1939 and Jack Benny with his family in 1940. Clark Gable and the then-actor Ronald Reagan were later guests. The three sister ships served as sets for movies such as: "Ma And Pa Kettle Go To Hawaii", Hitchcock's "Vertigo" with Kim Novak and James Stewart and "Golden Gate" during the familiar phone booth scene at Presidio Point.

In 1941 the USMC chartered the S.S. Monterey to collect refugees of Korea, Japan, China, several missionaries and stranded U.S. citizens and deliver them to San Francisco. Then she was stripped of her elegant sequined look and restructured for military duty which she began in World War II. In December of 1941 she sailed to Honolulu with thousands of soldiers and returned with 800 casualties. The U.S. Navy then sub-chartered her to embark Marines to Pago Pago. She returned to San Francisco with thousands of Army troops to sail to Brisbane in a convoy with the Matsonia built in 1927 and the Mormacsea.

She left New York twice, bound for Scotland in April of 1941, carrying thousands of troops.

It was November 6, 1942 when she boarded 6747 soldiers in New York, for a harrowing journey to Liverpool, Gibraltar and Naples. Twenty-five war planes accompanied the convoy which included the Grace Line's Santa Elena which was torpedoed and began to sink. The Monterey, at great risk to herself and her crew, sailed forward to rescue the 1675 soldiers. A lone bomber flew so low over the Monterey that a terrified soldier was able to hit it with the ship's anti-aircraft gun. The bomber plummeted into the sea, carrying part of the ship's radio antennae with it. Monterey continued full speed ahead sailing for Naples with her destroyer escort. A torpedo grazed her bow and glanced off. A near miss.

The Monterey joined another convoy transporting troops bound for Casablanca in North Africa in November 18, 1942. She carried injured soldiers back to the U.S. and was reassigned to carry 6855 troops to join a convoy for Oran.

In July 1944, as the Monterey was sailing the route of Milne Bay to Oro Bay, the skies darkened and visibility was reduced to zero from ash of a distant volcano. In spite of reduced speed and extreme caution, she ran aground. Thousands of military personnel disembarked; oil and water were dumped to lighten the load and she was freed from the embankment. Fortunately, there was no serious damage and she continued her service to the U.S. Government until 1946.

In the latter part of 1946, the Monterey began her conversion back to a luxury cruise liner. Low funds forced her sale to the U.S. Government and a lay up in Suisun Bay, close to San Francisco.

Good news arrived at a leisurely pace: it took nine years for the Monterey to be repurchased by Matson Lines. In 1955 she was towed to Newport News Shipbuilding & Dry-dock Company, while the naval architects firm of Gibbs and Cox, her original designers, began her facelift. She was redecorated with an Hawaiian flare. Ten feet were added to her superstructure and she was fitted for 761 first class accommodations. Her name had been given to a former cargo vessel that was also reconverted for deluxe passenger service in the South Pacific, so Monterey was renamed the Matsonia in May 1957. The next month she set sail once again from San Francisco to Los Angeles and to Honolulu.

As the Matsonia she sailed from 1957 until 1962 when she was laid up once again due to low sales. At the same time Lurline had major turbine damage and her repairs were too costly to be carried out. Lurline was sold to Chandris Lines of Greece and renamed the Ellinis - A blow to her past passengers. The Matsonia was renamed and christened as the new Lurline on December 6, 1963. She continued her sailing in the Hawaiian Islands with departures from San Francisco through Los Angeles. In May 1970 Matson sold their beloved Lurline to Chandris Lines who then renamed her the Britanis in June and set sail for Piraeus, Greece.

The Britanis was now refitted to house 1655 passengers. Several furnishings and bridge equipment from the Matson era were kept and displayed on a back deck in deference to her illustrious history.

February 1971 began her service from Southampton for three years. She then did winter Caribbean and summer European itineraries. It was in May of 1982 that Fantasy Cruises, a subsidiary of Chandris Lines, took over the Britanis, sending her on a New York to Bermuda run under Panamanian registry. Her capacity was reduced to 1200. After a major refitting with various parts from her sisters who have all been scrapped now, she returned to Miami, Florida for year- round Caribbean and Mexico cruises. A once- a- year cruise was added for seven consecutive years consisting of 47 to 50 days of the Circumnavigation around South America. This was to be a dramatic end to her career. It, however, was not.

I joined the ship in 1990 as assistant to Tommy Van, the Cruise Director. We were busy preparing for the third Circumnavigation cruise and enjoying the anticipation. The disembarking passengers were in tears.

The ship had molded them into a family and they were devastated at the thought of parting from each other.

I did some of the winter cruises and most of the summer ones. In 1991, I again did the Circumnavigation cruise. There were exciting ports of call, tough passengers and many daily activities. Shortly after returning to our Cozumel run, we had a large fire. Seventeen cabins were destroyed and fear spread quickly throughout the vessel. She had advantages over modern vessels in the quality of her construction and the loving care constantly given by her Greek officers.

She sailed her last 50-day Circumnavigation of South AmericaCruise in 1994. There was a hole in the bottom of the Britanis and that too, she survived.

Soon after her return, she was chartered by the U.S. Government to house military personnel in Guantanamo Bay, Cuba. Again, there was a fire, handled successfully by her devoted officers and crew. During all these voyages, she continued to run with her original engines.

As of November 1996 the Britanis has been laid up and put on the auction block. In January 1998, she was sold to AG Belofin Investments of Liechtenstein who wanted to scrap her in India or Pakistan. They renamed her the S.S. Belofin-1. Political unrest has caused a decrease in steel prices and plans have been put on hold. We who love her, hope that a California-based Majestic Group can negotiate to buy the Britanis. She would be refitted as a waterfront hotel in San Francisco. Once again she would be named the Lurline; preserving her proud heritage. It was tragic news when we learned in summer of 2000, that we had lost her, still loving her.

I thank Mr. Peter Knego, ship historian, journalist and good friend for putting the years and events in consecutive order and allowing me to recount the heroics and longevity of the Britanis - a special ship.

The Steamship Society boarded the Britanis to honor her spirit and commitment to U.S. history. While the Captain was tracing the history of the vessel in a speech, a gentleman stood and asked to approach the stage. The Captain graciously waved him over, not knowing what he might want to say. He wanted to say that he was the soldier who stood on the top deck with the antiaircraft gun listening for air approach. Without hesitation he had fired at the sound of something buzzing just to the side of his head. He had scored a hit and the bomber nose-dived to the sea, clipping the radio antennae on its way down. I had goose bumps on top of goose bumps as his story progressed. I could visualize a man, then in his prime, scared yet courageous, who saved the lives of the 1675 soldiers who would be rescued by this ship. The 6747 troops on board were also spared because of one soldier's action. I am sure that hero of the Britanis never imagined she would have sailed for more than 60 years.

I was standing at the entrance of the Ballroom one night when an elderly gentleman lay down on the floor, searching for something. I thought he had dropped something so I offered to help.

"No, young lady, something is just too familiar with this place and I can't place it."

"So, why are you on the floor."

"There," he yelled, "I knew it. See that round shape through the carpet over there?" I bent down and sure enough there was a round shape there. "Little lady, I was on this ship in 1942. She brought me back to the waiting arms of U.S. soil after I was wounded during my duty." He wept. With quiet emotion, he continued. "I walked around here for three days. Flashbacks I guess. Those round places there is where my bunk used to be. We were piled here three and sometimes four deep with injured and sick soldiers. I can remember thousands of us here praying to return home fast. We couldn't wait to see our moms and dads, sisters and brothers and be wrapped in their loving embraces. I will never forget it."

A man asked me how old the ship was. I told him it sailed in 1931. I also directed him to the information desk where there was a hand out sheet with the history and the prior names the vessel held. The next day, the man approached came to me with tears in his eyes, saying that the Monterey was the ship that took him to the Pacific for his first service. He said the ship was the last beautiful thing he enjoyed until his return five years later.

I well remember a family of four who boarded. The husband told me they were celebrating their twenty-fifth anniversary and wanted to spend it on a ship. They had honeymooned on a ship and their first daughter was conceived on that cruise. They were traveling with two daughters now. I asked what ship they had traveled. He said he thought it started with an 'L'.

I asked if it was "Lurline". "Yes, I think that is it." he said. "Well, sir, this is the old Lurline. This ship had several names over its history." The man began to weep. I asked him if he was okay and he said, "I'm sorry. This is really difficult to believe. You see, we came here together; probably for the last time. Our youngest daughter has cancer. Our eldest daughter is recovering from leukemia and is in remission. But my wife found out last week that she is terminally ill with cancer." I was emotionally overcome but I promised him to make his anniversary special.

We decorated a corner of the Bar with a sign that said, "Welcome home to the Lurline." The chef prepared a superb feast, including a decorated cake. The man blindfolded his wife and escorted her to a seat. We all sang Happy Anniversary. The wife was so thrilled with the meal she didn't notice the sign. I asked her again to read the sign. It still didn't register. I told her that she was on the ship of her honeymoon. She burst into tears and hugged everyone in sight.

Tommy, the Cruise Director and I stayed in our cabins one afternoon while the staff left to organize the beach activities. I was suddenly awake; there was a tapping at my porthole. I looked out but no one was there. There was noise in the next cabin. I opened my door and Tommy was standing there; annoyed at being awakened. The knocking at my porthole continued. We put our ears next to the glass, thinking the sound was from a vibration on the ship. The knock was far too loud. It was as if an invisible hand was knocking directly at us. Twenty minutes later it stopped. We settled down again in our beds. Moments later, we both opened our doors. We were sure there was a party in the hall and we yelled for quiet. But no one was there. We checked every staff cabin. They were all empty.

I was now spooked and told Tommy it was time for a triple dose of gin and tonic. It was and we did. We never told anyone about our experience, knowing they would call us loony.

Several times staff members quietly came to me to tell me a story about their roommates. Two dancers shared a bunked cabin. The dancer in the lower bunk claimed the girl above slapped her in the middle of the night. She asked her to stop, but she persisted. One night the girl jumped out of bed to hit her roommate back just as a young girl seemed to pass through the closed door. She wore a black dress, white apron and round white hat on her head, like a cabin stewardess of years past. She looked at the girls, turned and left. Both girls screamed, ran to my cabin and jumped onto my bed. I just laughed at their story and told them it could have been a ghost but that traditionally, ghosts don't slap people. The girls never forgot the incident.

A year later, with new dancers on board, this same story is repeated. Now what? These girls could not have talked with the others. They didn't know each other. Slowly, other stories surfaced - all involving the same girl, dressed exactly as the bunkmates had described. Passengers started asking about her. One said that he didn't see anything but that he felt the air in his room move as if someone had passed by his bed. He wasn't afraid, but it made the hair on his arms stand at attention. These incidents were spread throughout different cruises. There was no pattern to them. There were theories that the girl may have committed suicide on board or that she was jealous. That would explain the face slapping. There were also reports of a young child seen about the ship. No one could exactly describe the child, who would slip in and out of rooms like a proper ghost.

Our Stage Manager, Lynda Smith, kept her hat collection on her wall for convenience. Her favorite black hat was missing. I checked all the cabins. No luck. I called a meeting and asked if someone was pulling a joke. No one was. A new staff boarded and Lynda and I stayed on board to train them. Four days later, her hat was back exactly where it had always been. I was not guilty but who was?

On a weekend cruises from Miami to Nassau, Bahamas, a group of rowdy teenagers decided to play rough and tough. One of them came on to me while I was trying to get through the disco to an event in another room. I pushed him away telling him to sleep it off. Half an hour later, the dancers and I went to the disco to have a nightcap. Suddenly, someone broke a bottle over the bar counter and started chasing one of our bridge officers outside. Another began punching other passengers sitting quietly among friends. All hell broke loose. We girls ran. Security and other bridge officers came immediately and stopped the fighting. They took the boys to their cabins which had already been trashed. There were broken doors, broken glass, and scratched walls. They were put in their cabins until the next-morning arrival. The office was contacted we were told to do nothing but fine the boys for damages. They were fined $800.00 and free to do more damage. We were told one was a son of a New York Mafia leader - don't make waves. This gives permission to terrorize other passengers who paid to come on the ship for a good time? For the crew who worked there to have to fight like a gang on the streets? Personally I was livid. The next night, none of us girls came out to work. We remained in our cabins to have a private party. Meanwhile, the disco was handed over to the boys as they flew the records off the back deck like Frisbees in the sea and poured beer over the entire sound equipment. This additional damage they didn't pay for, the company did.

Next, we were chartered by the "Trekkie" fans of Star Trek and some of the cast cruised with us. These people knew how to party. They dressed in character every night. These wonderful people devote their earnings and their free time to meet fans, show off collectible merchandise and tell amusing stories. They are passionately involved in a harmless hobby. More people should be.

On one charter all the passengers were deaf. They communicated in sign language. It was awesome. The shows of music and dance still were performed for them. To show their appreciation, they didn't applaud but held their hands up high and waved them from side to side. The Las Vegas type show was new to them and they enjoyed it thoroughly. They were polite handsome people with a positive spirit and good will. I thank them for allowing us to be a part of their treasured memories.

On the following cruise a deaf girl came to me asking to be in the talent show. She wanted to sing. I was surprised but intrigued. She requested the band play "Wind Beneath my Wings." She asked me to look directly at her so she could lip read when I introduced her. The band started. She swayed with the music in perfect harmony and she interpreted the lyrics artistically by signing. One thousand passengers gave her a standing ovation.

In 1989, my life changed forever. I was told that I would be working on the Britanis. Neal Scott, a friend, was a dancer who was already there. We exchanged cassette letters. My friend Darlene and I listened as Neal spoke about the Social Hostess on board and her Staff Captain husband. He labeled them tough customers. Neal was willing to bet that I could have this girl for breakfast and put her in her place. I wasn't so sure but I told Darlene that I would marry the Staff Captain. Yes, I said it. I had never seen his picture, never even heard his name and didn't know him from Timbuktu. We laughed and that was the end of it.

The 47 day Circumnavigation cruise Around South America was days away. Darlene came to visit for the two days we loaded up supplies. I asked the Staff Captain's permission for her to visit the ship and he told me under the condition she comes to his cabin after. HA HA! A few days underway, I stopped the Staff Captain, offered my hand to shake and mentioned that we were never officially introduced. I was Joyce Gleeson, the Assistant Cruise Director. He said hello, but that he was shy. I said, "bullshit" and walked away. I wanted to die having said that. He really must have thought me weird.

I had been told this was the husband of the Social Hostess. Yet while he was on vacation she remained on board. It is odd for a Greek man to vacation without his wife. Also, she was having an affair. I warned the young man she was with to stay clear of the Staff Captain.

A few days later, I began to have difficulty with the Staff Captain's wife and he was suddenly flirting with me. Something was amiss. The telephone operator called saying the Staff Captain wanted to talk to me and connected us. I asked what he wanted and he said he didn't want to talk to me. I called the operator back and she said that he really wanted the Social Hostess. Her orders to the telephone operator were to put the Staff Captain through to the Cruise Director or the Assistant. I went to her cabin to get the story. She claimed he was bothering her by calling repeatedly. She wanted nothing to do with him. They were separated but she wanted to stay married because of better tax benefits. I told her not to involve me or other staff members in her onboard marital problems.

We had a great drink one afternoon; the Cruise Director, the Chief Purser, Staff Captain and me. "Screaming Orgasm" was its name. We drank this concoction while watching a silly computer game and we got just as silly as the game and much louder. What I hadn't realized was that the Social Hostess was standing in my room (which I left unlocked) She heard us howling with laughter. Jealousy is a dangerous weapon to wield.

The next day, I took inventory of the Staff Captain. He had been playing volleyball in a tiny black bathing suit, little black socks, and little black Reeboks. A towel draped over his shoulders and sweat pouring off his body. Oh, honey! Those thighs and tight buns were a smash hit for my tired aching eyes. But I told myself "No" because he was married.

It was formal night and I couldn't find my sequined gown. Frustrated and mystified, I put on another dress and left for my activity. I had sent a staff member back to my cabin to get an extra bottle of champagne. She reached for it from the bottom of my closet, and returned to tell me that my gown was on the floor behind the bottles. I was relieved until I saw the dress cut up in several slices. I discussed the situation with Tommy. We couldn't come up with a name until morning when the Social Hostess looked at me. No mystery then.

I went to her cabin to hash out the problem. I decided that she had delivered her report to my cabin and heard us having a wonderful time next door. What could her problem be? She was dating someone else and telling her separation story. I told her she had to wear the dress she had cut up at the next formal night or she would be off the ship. She complied and she hated me for it.

I told the Staff Captain that I couldn't handle his wife's behavior to me as well as the rest of the staff. Her nickname was "the barracuda". He politely informed me that he was not married and never had been. He had repeatedly asked her not to tell people that they were married.

I sat down. "So listen, when we get back to Miami in thirty-five days we could get married freely if you want."
"Yes, but I don't ever want to be married."

I told the Cruise Director about the marriage charade and that I wanted no part of it. We decided jointly to let the Social Hostess do her duties without paying any attention to her. This was difficult. The ship was small and the staff proportionate so there could be no shirking responsibility.

One night I was having a drink as I watched the show. The Chief Purser and Staff Captain sat on either side of me. At the end of the number, I playfully punched the Staff Captain telling him to applaud. He said he didn't know how. I punched him again after the next number and he told me to be careful, I might turn him on. I was grateful for the darkness because I blushed from head to toe.

At the end of the show, Tommy and the other hostesses, Geri, Donna and I dressed in 50's outfits for the theme night. We finished partying at 1:00 A.M. and were ready for a nightcap when the telephone operator found me. "The Staff Captain wants to speak with you." "Okay, put him on," I said.

"I hear you were a professional swimmer and know how to give a good massage."

"What? Yes, I know. Why?"

"You know where my cabin is?"

"Yes."

"Are you free?"

"Yes."

"Then come here." he hung up.

I stood there in shock not knowing what to do. He was a senior officer and you didn't annoy them in those days. I excused myself, claiming I was tired and I slipped upstairs to his cabin. I had vowed never to have an affair or marry an officer. I had seen the majority of officer's wives conducting themselves in a rude and snobbish manner. I didn't want to be like them.

I knocked, I walked in and there he was in bed. I laughed myself silly. I gave him the massage and we have been together ever since!

His point of view is different. It follows:

I have been on several ships during my career, but the majority of years have been with Chandris Lines. I started with them back in 1972. Three times, though, I had gone to other companies when they told me that after my vacation, they didn't have a position open for me. So for six months I found the Captain position on a cargo ship. Another time was for a few months on the Daphne and the other one on the Ocean Princess.

My time included several vessels with Chandris Lines, now called Celebrity Lines, those ships were: Patris, Ellinis, Australis, Victoria, Britanis, Azur, Horizon, Zenith, Meridian, Century, Galaxy, Mercury and Infinity to date.

One of my best memories was In 1975 when I was put on the Patris to sail to Darwin, Australia where the ship was used as a hotel for six months for those to use who were left homeless due to a cyclone that devastated their land. I found a regular girlfriend. A sweet-girl with fair skin, long brown hair and a cute figure. I adored her; we pleased each other in every way. She helped me to become fond of Australia: with the people, the land, the culture, the laid back style of life and the fun. One day I was playing volley with other crew when someone hit the ball out in the water. One of the boys dove in and went after it, even after he was told it was shark infested and the currents were dangerous and strong. He got stuck; he couldn't get back, so I dove in to get him. Once he was back, I thought to myself, 'oh, go ahead and get the ball it isn't that hard.' When I got the ball, I suddenly realized where I was. I had to concentrate hard, relax, not swim in panic, take my time and find my way back. Risky challenges are only done when you are young and not thinking.

I continued on ships making my money, enjoying the world, having my fun (though I don't tell of my affairs, I answer what my wife asks of me, but I have always felt strongly that these are private matters with no reason to try to make an impression).

When I was working on the Ocean Princess, again I had found a steady girlfriend. Being a sailor in uniform it isn't difficult to get a woman. But I always preferred to be with one woman at a time, unless between girlfriends as it made for less chance of spreading diseases. When the time came for me to go back onto a Chandris ship I had told my girlfriend to try to get on. When I arrived on the Britanis, there she was.

Time with her however, was getting more and more difficult. I wanted to remain with her but her attitude was hard to deal with. Not saying that I am any easier but I asked her several times not to tell people that we were married, because it was not true. I also asked her to stop telling others about the intimacies between us. Being rash and demanding in her ways made me annoyed and tired. I wanted a quiet relationship with quiet time, no screaming, no fighting and no explaining. Asking too much maybe, but this is simply what I wanted.

Vacation was coming up now and I told her that it was best that we separate for the three months. I would be gone and for her not to come to Greece with me. I was nervous at the time for I rented a house in Piraeus with my mother and we were in a position of having to move because the owners wanted their place back. I would be busy and did not want to deal with her. As it happened, I had to rush to buy a house, which I understand Americans call an apartment, because my mother was crying every day that she would be on the street when I went back to the ship. I rushed into purchasing a two-bedroom house without seeing it, for it was not completely built, and went back to the ship. I paid cash; that is the only way we know to get something we need, so going back to the ship was a necessity to get some money back into the bank.

Upon arriving, I found out that my ex-girlfriend was still there and she was confirmed to do the 47-day Circumnavigation South America Cruise. I wasn't happy about it but since there was nothing I could do, I tried to contact her to let her know I would be there as a friend, nothing more. I also knew already that she was with someone else. However, each time the telephone operator put me through to the Assistant Cruise Director. I didn't understand, but so what. I tried several times but without success. I gave up not really caring.

The Assistant Cruise Director walked up to me one day throwing out her hand to introduce herself "officially". Under my breath I hadn't cared we were not introduced "officially." But what to do? I shook her hand, telling her I was shy. She told me "bullshit" and walked away. She made me laugh.

After watching her for a couple of weeks, I was told about her one night while I was sitting in the Ballroom with the Shore Excursion manager Roy, a character all his own. We watched her as she walked in to do an activity. Roy had pointed out that she was probably the best one on the ship for this two and a half-month cruise we had embarked on. We were both single, so why not?

One night I decided to try my luck. With self-confidence I waited until her late activity was finished and called her through the operator. She sounded aloof or maybe surprised. I'm not sure which, but she agreed to come up. She

76

Egypt 1985. The infamous runaway camel.

Christmas 1986 S. Oceanis. Typical greek dance.

"It's Magic" Mr. Blackwell.

Summer 1986. Ramona Hennessey, the author and actress Barbara Rush.

The Britanis in South America.

We loved the Britanis so much we ate it.

From the chill of Alaska, USA to

the chill of Tierra del Fuego, South America.

From the heat of the Panama Canal, Panama to

the heat of the Corinth Canal, Greece.

Famous spiritual rock visited by Shirley MacLaine
in Machu Picchu, Peru.

South America. Patagonia penguin life.

Peruvian splendor.

ECK... We touched rear ends but he spit first. Cusco, Peru.

If I were not upon the sea.

quietly knocked on the door. I jumped in bed to see her reaction when she walked into the door.

"You're in no doubt shy, aren't you?"

"Well, I asked you to come here to give me a massage."

"So, what makes you so sure that I would come."

"I really didn't. With the little flirting the last few days, I thought I would try. And here you are. So give me massage."

We have been together ever since. That was in 1990.

Just a few days after we started dating we arrived in Puerto Madryn. Across the pier I had spotted some sea lions taking a morning break. I talked Joyce into walking with me down close to where they lay. They were sleeping so we would be okay. Just as we got close, I picked Joyce up from behind and pretended to throw her on one of the animals. She let out a scream, woke one up and we froze while waiting to see what it was going to do. It completely ignored us and went back to sleep.

Most of time has been spent together. Two or three times we were separated because of duties to complete on other ships. Our lives are unusual with all our travels, but Joyce is constant in her ways to push me, though at times it has been difficult and I've become very angry with her, we seem to find the next step to move forward.

Chapter Seven
The Passenger Chronicles

I was sitting at the Hostess desk one afternoon. A man came up to me and said,

"Hi, Joyce, How are you?"

"Hi, Bill. I'm doing great."

Wait a minute. How did I know his name? Of course, he knew mine from reading my name tag. I looked down and my name tag wasn't there. I looked up; surprised. He said,

"Don't worry. We knew each other in a past life. You know what Joyce, you have a lot of dreams that you can't answer, don't you. Make sure you write them all down. One day you will meet the person who will explain what they all mean. Until then, let us have some fun."

During the two-week cruise, Bill mentioned that the wind blew his hat away.

"Hold on." I went with him to the lost and found box in the Purser's office and grabbed one of 11 hats. I handed him a hat that indeed was his. "It's impossible the hat was found," he said, "because I watched it fly off into the water." I explained, "Obviously the wind caught hold of it, blowing it back on a lower deck." I never figured out how I knew which hat was his but he was happy to have it back. They had been together 40 years. Nearly 16 years later, we are still writing each other. Each time he sends me a letter, I have sent him one on the same date. No explanation - it just is.

Because of the length of the South American cruise, we had very little gambling. We closed half of the casino and made the other half into a small cinema for those who could not easily get to the regular cinema. It was a day at sea and we had a packed house. Two center seats were available, one directly behind the other. A tall gentleman took one of the seats. Shortly afterward, an even taller gentleman took the seat in front of him. The man in the rear now couldn't see the screen. He leaned forward and asked, "Please move your chair."

He did, but not enough to satisfy the first man.

"Move, or else."

"Move your own chair."

A slap on the head to the man in front and suddenly they were both up walloping each other. Seeing two seventy-eight year-olds fighting as ten-year olds was hilarious. Their movements were in slow motion when they needed fast forward. They gave each other bloody noses and plenty of scratches before the Cruise Director dared to get in between them.

The fight over deck chairs is a long running classic. Most passengers seem to want to bask in the sun all day long. The first round consists of getting a chair close to the pool. Leaving the chair, however briefly, will result in the chair being occupied and belongings placed on the deck by an alert usurper. Round two begins.

Some trudge, with chair, through doors and around waiters and fellow passengers, to the security of their cabin: thus prepared to set up camp when dawn breaks. Even if they are booked for an all-day tour that next day they can go in peace. They know where their deck chair is. Watching them getting the chair into the elevator is spectator sport. When the door opens, they look around, distressed, and complain loudly that they "can't fit the chair in with all these people". The sight is so unorthodox that many times stunned passengers will clear the elevator for the furniture movers. The cabin steward always takes the chair back to the deck and begins again...

There are students and teachers in the "Get More Than Ten Meals a Day" (after all, you paid for it). This is structured and the ritual must be followed exactly as prescribed.
1. Order continental breakfast in cabin.
2. Proceed to restaurant for full breakfast.
3. Go to deck buffet.
4. Visit table with muffins and coffee machine before leaving deck.
5. Return to restaurant for luncheon.
6. Return to upper deck for pool side buffet.
7. Collect full plate of cakes and sandwiches at tea time, munch on mounds of crackers served with pre dinner drinks.
8. Order from all four courses of the dining room menu.
9. Sample offerings from the midnight buffet.
10. Eat all fruit from basket in cabin.

Enough is never enough for some. On disembarkation mornings I often saw passengers carrying off their souvenir gift bag stuffed with miniature cereal boxes. I asked a woman why she was doing this and she announced that the company owed it to her because she paid the price to come on the cruise. Oh???

Another woman wanted to stock up so that she didn't have to go to the store for a few days. Yet another pointed out that with four children, the cereal would be breakfast for a few days. She paid for the cruise so she was going to get her money's worth. Yes, and then some. However bizarre their rationale, they believe it.

It is fast becoming rare to find the person who just enjoys their surroundings. Many times, a passenger collects complaints at boarding and takes them along as constant companions for every day of the cruise. Passengers will come on board with the same problem they were trying to escape. We had a sad incident with a California police officer, who understandably needed a vacation. I commend police and firefighters for putting their lives at stake. They are too often taken for granted. The officer tried constantly to relax, rethink his life and step out of his problems, which included divorce proceedings. Yet, five days later, his unstable mind snapped. He broke up his cabin, damaging the mirror, the bathroom door, the cabinet drawers and a chair. When the ship's officers came to stop what they thought was a fight, they found him alone and distraught. He asked them to put him in a straight jacket because he was afraid of what he might do to himself or others. They did as he asked. An ambulance met him at the next port and although we never heard a report, we hoped for his suffering to end.

We had a nice young single male passenger traveling with us on the next two-week cruise. He didn't bother anyone; he remained aloof. He went out in the ports during the day and sat at the bar during the evenings; not getting drunk, just staying quiet. We had just heard that President Reagan had ordered the bombing of Libya. Passengers were ecstatic and proud. I walked over to the young man and asked him his thoughts, just to have a conversation with him. He chuckled, "It really isn't much."

"Well", I said, "most here are happy about it but I know nothing of politics and war. What do you think?"

"Listen, I don't go around telling people what I do, however, I'm here on a much needed vacation, a bit incognito. I am a member of the swat team."

"Wow, I've never met anyone on the swat team. What do you do?"

"I'm not at liberty to give details, but we clean up the dirty work."

"Well then, why doesn't the United States just get in there and take out Kadhafi?"

"Listen, think about it. We could go in there now and take him, but there isn't a reason to. It took years to be able to decode their information. If we get rid of him, then it will take that many more years to start all over, decoding with a new leader in. It is better to leave well enough alone. We are able to stop ninety-nine percent of bomb attacks, assassination attempts and more. There are just a few that get through us and those are the ones you hear about. You will never know about those we caught. Remember the bomb at the German disco? We were minutes away from stopping it. More lives are saved rather than lost by us knowing these codes."

"Gee, I never thought of it that way. You see? I really don't know much about it, that's probably better. We have to trust those in your position to save our lives and our interests."

I've thought often of that man when hearing of a bomb attack or an arrest of a known terrorist. I wonder what he thinks of Osama Bin Laden? There is a scary person. I never heard of a sect that states that it is 'their religion' to kill Americans.

The most humorous incident I can remember took place in St. Lucia in the West Indies. I was talking with an adventuresome couple wanting to take local transportation to the Soufriere Volcano. I explained the two different types of taxis. Those belonging to the taxi association of the island and those outside the gates who don't. They selected one outside the gates. The driver was friendly and excited to be chosen. They had to travel the long route, crisscrossing the island because the road on the shorter route was washed out. They made it there and halfway back. The driver was distraught when his car broke down at a spot overlooking a cliff. He vowed to deliver his passengers to the ship at no extra cost. He told them to wait; he had a friend who owned a boat at the bottom of the cliff. He climbed down and to his good fortune, his friend was there. He climbed back up and waved them to follow him down. The thought of missing the ship inspired their descent. The driver was desperate to make a good impression on the visitors and it wasn't going well. Into the boat they went.

I was pool side conducting the afternoon quiz. The ship was just about underway when we heard a funny chug-chug sound along the side of the ship. Looking over, we saw our two passengers in an authentic hollowed out log. A tiny motor was attached with a thick white rope on the back - they were bailing water out with their shoes, and yelling for the ship not to sail. They made it on board two minutes before the gangway was lifted. We were all hysterical at the scene. As they approached the pool area to get a stiff drink, everyone on deck gave them a standing ovation. I handed them the microphone and let them tell their story. As we sailed out of the harbor, all on deck saluted the island of St. Lucia, in gratitude, appreciation and in memory of the little cab that could.

My friends Neal and Darlene and I pooled our money to buy a TV/VCR. We would watch videos in my cabin until very early in the morning. Mine was the last passenger cabin before the staff accommodations. One night we were intent on the video when someone walked in and peed on my life jacket that I had left on the floor. Here was a man of about 6' 5", naked and staring straight ahead into my mirror. After the male ritual, he left. There was no security then, so I called for the night steward STAT. The three of us watched as the man casually walked down the hall. The night steward passed him without a glance and asked us what we wanted. I told him to turn around and look. "Oh, I'll see what I can do," he said, casually. We went back to my cabin howling with laughter when my phone rang. The operator told me that an hysterical woman was reporting a strange man in her cabin. I took the passenger list and we three ran towards her cabin. I found the woman in the hall in distress. I explained who I was and offered help. She said there was a naked man sitting next to her husband on his bed. As we approached the cabin, the intruder was on his way out. It was so late at night, we decided to straighten everything out in the morning. Suddenly, Neal yelled that the man was going into the elevator. I ran to the elevator, pulled him out, while Darlene tried to calm the woman.

"Sir, excuse me. What is your name?"

"The same as it was yesterday!"

"Well, I didn't know your name yesterday. Could you help me today?"

"Well, look it up in the phone book!"

Good thing that I had taken my passenger list, "Look, sir. I have the phone book of the ship. Tell me your name and I can find your address and cabin number."

"Oh okay then, it's _____ Thank you, here it is. Are you traveling with your wife, _____ "Well I went to bed with her, didn't I?"

"I sure hope so, but sir, your cabin is on the other side. Why don't we go together!"

I knocked on the cabin door, but no answer. I asked the night steward to open it. I walked in, turned on the light and saw a woman sleeping in the bed next to the porthole. I quietly called her name but she didn't answer. I thought she might not have her hearing aid on, so I yelled louder. She jumped up. I explained who I was and that her husband had gotten lost. She apologized, saying she feared this would happen; he had Alzheimer's. I felt sad for him. I told her that he must have been trying to locate the bathroom but he opened the wrong door and locked himself out. My door was open. When he walked in and saw himself in the mirror, he thought he was in his own bathroom. I advised her to leave a chair in front of the door for the rest of the cruise so that he wouldn't get out. We informed the Chief Purser and Captain of the problem the next morning. They called the other passengers to apologize and explain the circumstances. The next night, he got out again. This time two entertainers found him and corralled him, then called me. I went to his cabin, got his pants and his wife. Obviously, she had not used the chair suggestion.

The next day, the Captain asked the doctor to check the man out. The wife's story changed; she claimed her husband had a patch behind his ear for seasickness, which made him crazy. The Captain was mad at me for what he perceived as a lie relating to the Alzheimer's story: I was mad at the doctor. He had not actually seen the passenger; only spoken to him on the phone. I explained that there was no patch behind his ear either time I saw him. Each time, I tried to focus on his head to avoid looking down. I would have noticed the Scopolamine patch. The wife was ashamed so she invented excuses for her husband's aberrant behavior. I told her not to be silly and that we would help her find a solution. She started using the chair and there were no more escapes.

On another ship, my husband and I had a woman visitor at two A.M. I jumped out of bed. My husband was groggy and non comprehending. I put my pants on and went into his office. There was a woman sitting at his desk.

"Excuse me, can I help you?" I asked.

"I want my cabin. I'm lost."

"I'm sorry. What is your cabin number."

"I don't know. It isn't written on my card, which they tell me is also my key. Listen, can I use your bathroom I really need to pee."

"Excuse me, do you know you are in the Captain's office and you walked into his cabin?"

"No, please, I really need to use his bathroom."

"Ma'am, you can not. Please, give me your key. I will call the operator."

"Hello, this is the Captain's wife. I have a woman who is lost. This is her name. Can you please give me her cabin number so I can get her to there."

"Oh, excuse me, I helped this woman get dressed tonight. I think she doesn't understand where she is. She is always lost. Her cabin is..."

"Thanks, I will get her taken care of."

"Ma'am, your cabin is just outside here. Let me take you there."

"Thank you dear. You see I don't know where I am, this isn't my home. My daughter is supposed to be with me but she's not." She talked incessantly.

"So, how did you get here?"

"I don't remember. I don't remember many things. Where are we now?"

"You are on a ship in the Caribbean, Ma'am. Do you live in Florida?"

"Yes, I think so, but I'm not quite sure."

"Will someone pick you up tomorrow?"

"I don't know."

I put her in her cabin. I got up early the next morning to explain to the Social Hostess what had happened and to make sure that someone picked her up. She did live in Florida. Her daughter was afraid to travel with her, so she left her on the ship and got off. She did pick her up and take her home.

A similar incident happened on the Halley's Comet cruise when a grandson left his grandfather on board for 14 days. The elderly gentleman had not lost his memory. He was, however, incapable of bathing, dressing or feeding himself. He could talk and walk and little else. He wet the bed. He had few clothes, no medications and no one to help him. The stewards all pitched in daily: they bathed him, dressed him, fed him and washed his clothes. The rest of us welcomed him on tours and made sure he was seated for lectures, evening shows and bingo.

When we arrived in San Juan, the grandson was waiting. I chewed him up one side and down the other for his lack of responsibility let alone human compassion. The man didn't deserve the neglect he got from his grandson. I reminded the young man that he would not be alive except for his grandfather. Where was the respect due a human being, let alone a family member. Yes, it is wretchedly hard to take care of someone like this, but you must do it.

On a cruise out of Venice, Italy, our cabin was located next to the pool. I had just finished a tough workout and stripped down to take a shower, when three German women walked into the cabin and stood laughing at me. I screamed, "Close the door." Shaken, I got into the shower thinking they had left. Wrong! I could hear them laughing in my husband's office. I couldn't imagine how people could walk into what was obviously an office and sniff around at will. I jumped out of the shower, covered myself and found one sitting at his desk looking through his papers, one on the couch talking and the other opening the cabinet and the refrigerator. I couldn't speak German, but my face translated the message. They walked out giggling.

Two cruises later a group of four Italian men did the same thing, however, they apologized most graciously and went on their way without rifling through my husband's papers.

There is always an on board curiosity. People think a sign reading, "Private" doesn't apply to them. Many think that since they paid for the cruise, they have a right to search the vessel for their amusement. They ignore the fact that the ship is both home and office to those who work on board. Many have asked us what we do for our real jobs. Well...

Several years back, I had met a woman who was a child survivor of the Titanic. She didn't want the ship brought to the surface; she wanted her father, mother and two brothers to rest in peace. She remembered the cold; consequently, she hates cold weather. She remembered the silence after the ship sank; she doesn't like to be alone. It was years before anyone told her the story of why her family was taken from her. She was a strong and sensitive woman.

Later however, I was told by another friend, who traveled with her on another ship, that she went along with Titanic enthusiasts to view 'bringing up the Titanic'. She had hoped for closure. The equipment broke and the section went back to rest. She told everyone that it wasn't meant to be and to let it go. She passed away shortly afterwards.

A tiny green eyed woman was dancing with the captain. She was smiling, poised and showed no trace of the five years of horror she had survived 40 years past. She lost a husband, all four children and the brother who moved her from Russia safe house by safe house - and eventually by steamship to Canada and a train to the States. In 1986 she was on the cruise celebrating her 94th year. How I wish I could see her again on the dance floor.

We received the dreaded phone call one afternoon - Two passengers were fighting. Entering their cabin, we noticed that they had consumed a lot of alcohol ashore. He told her to get lost and she went berserk. She broke the mirror in the cabin then chased and sliced him several times. He retaliated by breaking a bottle of cologne and cutting her. When the shouting and banging became too loud, someone called security. They stopped the fight, called the doctor and put them in separate cabins until arrival in home port the next day.

Two men who were strangers were sharing a cabin. They were traveling with their company which was conducting a seminar at sea. The one man complained to the coordinator that his roommate had threatened him with a knife and acted weird. That night, that same passenger banged on the door of the bridge demanding to see the Captain. The officer on duty saw the knife he was carrying in the video viewer and called security. Thank God they arrived quickly because the office and our cabin were directly behind him. I shudder to think about it. He was disembarked at the next port.

Sometimes passengers are looking for ways to sue the company.

Three of us were having a morning coffee. We watched a woman walk in from the pool area, glass in hand, step off the carpet runner and proceed to make a puddle of water on the floor by dumping the contents of her glass. She turned and marched back out. Instinctively, my antennae stood 'up'. I called our ship's photographer. Five minutes later, she came back in with her friend, who had a camera in hand. She walked off the runner, her heel slipped on the puddle and she fell. Her friend started taking pictures. I called the doctor just as the photographer came. I told him to take pictures of the amateur photographer and the "Victim" on the floor. They screamed at him asking what he was doing. I walked over explaining that since she conveniently fell and had her friend take pictures, we were conveniently doing the same thing. The joke in the end was on her, she actually broke her leg. She received nothing because we witnessed the set-up.

Another woman greatly disappointed me. I had spoken with her often throughout the cruise. She was chaperoning, with two other teachers, a group of high school students. Late one evening she came to tell me that she had been attacked. When she told me it was her cabin steward, I was alarmed. He had been my steward. I knew he would never jeopardize his new promotion. I asked her if she was absolutely sure. Privately, I wondered why he would choose a heavyset middle aged woman over the many attractive young girls on board.

According to her claim report he had walked into her cabin and shut the door; she got scared and ran out. Where then, was the site of the attack? The next day she and another woman with her were loudly insisting that the steward be taken off the ship immediately.

Our lawyers came instantly. This incident allegedly occurred in the morning and she reported it 12 hours later. Also, she participated in a morning event I conducted within minutes of the "attack" and she hadn't seemed upset. Okay, all papers signed - end of story. Then one of her colleagues refuses to testify because he has to work with her. He confides that she made up the story to get something out of the deal. We knew that: proving it was the problem.

The steward could not work on board again until the case was litigated. There were three years of many more affidavits claiming psychiatric problems, inability to work, to perform wifely duties and then the story was rewritten by the plaintiff. The steward had torn her clothes off, had climaxed on her leg in his excitement at the prospect of intercourse. If her first round of accusations was preposterous, this version was disgusting. She was never attacked. She planned to get a free cruise. The steward's future was destroyed. He had worked for the company seven years, was married with five children and couldn't find a job because of the publicity. He didn't have the money to counter sue. Women who truly need help don't get it because of those who abuse the system for personal gain. It infuriates me.

There is another type of charge I can not accept. Two women were in line for the information desk. The person ahead of them was there for quite a long time. One of the women said, "Jeez, that girl is taking a long time with her because she don't want to serve no African American."

What?" I couldn't stay out of this one, "What does that girl helping that person have anything to do with your color. Please don't start that bull here; we don't have that problem. Leave that complaint for someone who is truly discriminated against. Not here; on this ship everyone gets top service, it doesn't matter who you are." She was real quiet real fast.

One of the managers finished a talk on stage. She alternated answering questions when two lines formed. For a second she answered a quick question of an elderly Asian woman before turning to another passenger. The woman went to the information desk to complain that because she was black, she was discriminated against by the manager who helped the other woman first. Bad choice. The manager was an adoptive mother to a black child.

I was once partially hypnotized by a passenger who became a good friend. Carol Manning was traveling with her father when I met her. During our talks she mentioned she could hypnotize. Out of curiosity, I asked her to hypnotize me. She did. I was aware of everything around me but I spoke in a male voice with a foreign accent. I felt frozen in place. My cousin Sharon was a witness to the session. I said things I was afraid to verbalize consciously. I complained that something at the base of my throat bothered me. To this day, I can neither wear a shirt, a sweater, nor a necklace over that spot. Carol told me that it was something in my life I had to investigate. As soon as I worked it out, that pressure would go away. I am intrigued but it gives me the "willies."

I was hosting a table with the Staff Captain. It was the Farewell party with the traditional parade of the baked Alaska. The liquid fire was accidentally poured on a woman's back. Flames shot up quickly. Instantly, both the Staff Captain and I jumped over two sets of chairs to cover her with our napkins. I escorted her to the doctor's office. Damage assessment: her hair slightly singed; both her pink silk blouse and her back sustained spotty superficial burns. As I left the office I saw the poor waiter sitting there. His hand was wrapped in a bloody linen napkin. When he lifted the napkin, I rushed back in the office. I asked the lady to please excuse us but the waiter was seriously injured. She told me he could be seen when she was finished. I explained that he needed immediate treatment because he was burned to the bone involving his muscles and nerves. She said he should have thought about that when he dropped it.

I was practicing my Italian language with a young honeymoon couple for the first few days at sea. We were at the pool when the Signor asked me to please come to their cabin. He wanted to give me something for my kindness. The Signora said to go without her, she wanted to continue sunning. When we got to the cabin, I stayed outside but he urged me to come in while he located the gift. I walked in as he slammed the door shut, put his arms around me and sensually kissed me. He lowered me on the bed, fondling me. Mama Mia! I gently pushed him away, thanked him for the compliment but said I had no intention of involving myself in their new marriage. He told me it was okay. I told him it wasn't. I had to be careful because you never knew when someone would go back to the company making up lies just to get even for being rejected. I told him under other circumstances I wouldn't hesitate but I liked his wife and didn't handle guilt well. He accepted my explanation - thank goodness. If he forced the situation, how could I explain my presence in his cabin? I never set foot in a passenger cabin again without an escort of some kind. That was 13 years ago. Today, a similar situation would be handled not between the two people but their attorneys.

Over the years, I remain in contact with several persons whom I have enjoyed and who have had an impact on my life. Ann Henkins was her name. She unfortunately passed away in 1995. She was a sweet beautiful woman, who had several surgeries on her throat so her voice was harsh yet intriguing. She was one of the original Rockettes and still had the body to prove it. I had the privilege to sail with her on four South America cruises where she kept me entertained with stories of her life. She didn't have children but had a nephew, James, whom she adored. He treated her like the special person she was. Ann had nothing to complain about, always had a kind word to say about everyone and was appreciative of the kindness we showed her. We dressed her up in show costumes every year to keep her memories of her stage days alive.

Ada Kauder is very hard to describe. She is wonderfully tough and the opposite of Ann Henkins. I sailed with her numerous times including seven 50-day South America cruises, as well as several other cruises in and out of New York. She is one of those people who becomes totally immersed in whatever interests her at the time. She was one of the first women to enlist in the military during WWII. She married twice, had no children, practiced Judaism and loves to harass anyone who will let her. Most let her. One day she appeared framed at the Captain's porthole in a ridiculous hat. That the Captain was conducting a meeting merely inspired her to pose and then to invite herself to the meeting.

A Yiddish word best describes Ada: kvetch. It translates as a chronic complainer, which she was, even about nice weather. She wasn't allowed off the ship before tour participants (who always had time restrictions to avoid missing the ship's departure). Why couldn't she get off? She had been on enough tours to write the definitive book on them but still - why couldn't she get off?

Kvetching is a fine art and Ada practiced it without prejudice. I was therefore not exempt from criticism even though we are friends. Passengers watched her in amazement. She would criticize everyone in her line of fire. One year she found a target she couldn't hit - Kissing Annie. She couldn't stand her. Kissing Annie ignored Ada, which really irritated her. She never let her out of her sights, though, and Annie's every action, speech and clothes selection was subject to attack by Ada. It was amusing to watch. Each of those women was delightful; especially in action. Ada calls herself the 'recycled teenager'. She keeps her self-esteem high. At 89 years young, I give credit where credit is due. She is solo on walks, bus rides, shopping, cruise vacations and never tires of harassing others. I cherish our friendship.

Broadway Joe flew from New York to Miami every month for two years to travel with us. He never ventured off in port; however, he seemed to live for the talent show. He always told the same jokes, sang the same songs and we never tired of him. It was inevitable that he would some day not appear on board. We never forgot him.

Mildred joined us for the four-day cruise to Mexico every three weeks. Her husband would always drop her off at the check-in counter and slowly walk away getting back to his car. He was there on time to pick her up. She enjoyed the meals, remained on board and always was the first one to get a front row seat for the shows. She would applaud with such enthusiasm we wanted to record her to hype up those who sat with stony stares at the performances.

One of my best friends, Carol Cohen, along with her husband Lew and kids, Matt and Albert, traveled with me on the Britanis. One night Albert appeared at his parents' cabin door. There was a man in his room trying to put on his pants. The passenger was sleep walking in his underwear and had settled in the boys' cabin. Carol went to the cabin, explained the mistake and the man turned and walked away.

I remember one time when my husband and I came back on board. We had to have a passenger cabin temporarily. Two male Spanish speaking passengers used their key, walked in our cabin, turned on the light and stood there staring at us. I jumped up! My husband explained that they were in the wrong cabin. They left, a bit confused but they left.

We were on our way to La Guaira, Venezuela when a couple of men were having drinks with the band vocalist and me. One of them was a former policeman from New Jersey. He told us how his family was going to help him smuggle $80,000.00 worth of drugs back to the States. His friend, who had traveled with us before, was trying to talk him out of it. We told him that the U.S. would not help him if caught. In addition, in Venezuela they physically tormented those who got involved with drugs. I explained that most of the time it was a set up with the same bag of drugs going around from dealers, to buyers, to police and back to dealers. They got their drugs back; they shared the money and 'you' were in jail. He didn't want to listen; nothing would dissuade him.

I was on the gangway as the passengers were boarding, when his friend, head down and obviously shaken, walked on I asked where his friend was and he pointed to the bottom of the gangway. The police had him and wanted his belongings from the ship. He was in serious trouble for years to come. We knew this from witnessing a horrendous scene involving a crew member a few months before. He was beaten senseless in front of our eyes at this port. There was NOTHING we could do. I cried. We were told not to interfere. He was dealing in drugs and a search of his cabin produced a stash of even more. He had kept his secret from all on board. When he tried to resist arrest upon entering the ship terminal, the police decided to make him an example of their zero tolerance policy. I had never seen anyone beaten like this. It was a hideous sight that I can not seem to forget.

Drug dealing can cost your freedom and in some countries, your life. The compassion and second chance policy exists in the States. Other countries have neither the mercy nor the patience.

I was on the ship during two bad hurricanes: David and Hugo. During David we had to go cabin to cabin securing passengers on their cabin floors with their bed mattress pushed alongside. In the lounge, the baby grand piano detached, slid off the bandstand and flew out the window. The bridge window cracked. We were not even in the middle of the storm but the periphery. Most passengers were scared but some thought of it as a game. Frankly, I wasn't amused. Those who were, rolled from one side of the ship to the other. A man in his seventies was actually doing somersaults several times before he lay down and laughed himself silly. I thought he had nipped some vodka but he was sober. He told me that he had already had a life - so it didn't matter now what happened. I countered that I hadn't had a long life and it certainly did matter what happened. He told me not to fret; he had been through this before and all would be fine. He was correct. I was amazed at his self confidence and the fun that he insisted upon having. Most of us were trembling and relieved when it was over.

Hugo - another kind of devastation. We had dodged four smaller hurricanes the week before, changing ports each time to avoid the storm. After all that maneuvering, we could have just as well gone on our normal run. Each hurricane changed its original path. We had just left Venezuela. We sailed slowly as Hugo was making his way north as were we. The Captain kept a vigilant watch in case Hugo changed his mind by looping around us. Hugo did not change course; he gained momentum. We rocked and rolled but still avoided meeting him up close and personal. News arrived that San Juan was badly damaged. This was our destination, so we had to remain out at sea for a couple of days, as there was an emergency situation on the island. Half the airport control tower was destroyed, a DC10 was damaged on the runway, which was itself damaged. Thousands were homeless, the power was out, the National Guard was called out to protect the streets. There were no Immigration Officers to clear the vessel and no pilots to bring us in.

The Captain held a meeting announcing in each passenger's language, his decision about our future course. The Venezuelans were so angry they demanded to know where the Captain got his license to drive. We all gasped. Historically, the Master is concerned with the safety of all on board. To question his intent or his expertise in a crisis situation is unthinkable. The Captain quietly put the microphone down on the stage floor and walked out.

Passengers were livid that we hadn't pulled alongside sooner. The Captain, without authority and at great risk, sailed the ship into port and docked us safely at the pier, just to make those who were angry - happy. We could not get off; the gates of the terminal were locked. Kids tried to climb over the gate to get to us for food, water and ice. The streets were wild. The police were out in force.

Although the passengers could see what was happening right in front of their eyes, several mentioned that they had better see some destruction to make their delay worthwhile. Who would want to see 25,000 people without home, food or clothing? Some wanted written notes from the Captain to give to their bosses for missing work. We told them to just show their cruise ticket and the itinerary for proof. Others had accused the Captain and staff of making up the hurricane story, as a coverup for the fact that our ship's engines were faulty and old. Some wanted a full refund because their cruise was interrupted. They received three extra days of free room and board plus food and drink because no one could get off. Some asked if we could sail to Miami so they could catch a plane home as San Juan airport was closed. We didn't have any more fuel, there was nobody to give us fuel. A hurricane just devastated everything in its path - did anyone understand this?

Providentially we then had the ship chartered by nearly seven hundred Carney owners; circus personnel know how to party. They enjoyed having entertainment provided rather than providing it. Masquerade night was unique because their costumes were unusual and filled with surprises. Their stories were funny and fast paced. These were Pros.

I was practicing my Italian with a family named Zucchini. They were a sister and brother along with her husband. The brother had never married. We all enjoyed each other's company. One night in the disco after the midnight buffet a man fell to the floor. I ran to help. I saw that it was Mr. Zucchini. A dancer and singer from the show started CPR while we notified our medical team and cleared the room. They tried for an hour to revive him but could not. His sister understandably cried and was shocked. We took her to her cabin and sedated her to keep her calm. Her husband attended to all the arrangements. Just before she fell asleep she told me that her brother was the one who was helping their father when he had perfected the human cannonball. She felt an era had disappeared. And she was right. The Carneys, however, continued to party in the style they knew he would want; I felt sad but they reminded me that it was better for him to die here with his friends partying than to be at home alone.

An African American group charter provided us with one of the best times we ever had. They were friendly, energetic, appreciative and a pleasure to see. They brought on their own entertainment. The sounds of Blues and Jazz reminded us of how music can elevate life; while Ashford and Simpson brought back the treasured sounds of the 50's and 60's to a standing roaring crowd. This was a delightful celebration. Each night we sat mid ship and watched the passengers amble by. These passengers dressed to the nines and remained dressed until they retired. The majority of cruisers today dress for dinner, then change to jeans for the show. My hat is off to each passenger on that special cruise who took us out of our routine and brought soul on board for us.

The Drifters boarded for the next cruise. I attended their concert and invited them to the bridge as we sailed. Each member was appreciative of the honor and thrilled as it was a first for them. As we were leaving, we were serenaded acapella by the group. None of us who were on the bridge that day will forget that wonderful sound.

The beautiful Barbara Rush has sailed with us as well as her son and sister. She is a fabulous woman with fans from the States to Turkey. When she shopped in the Grand Bazaar of Istanbul, hordes of fans recognized her from the popular Flamingo Road Series. To thank me for a favor to her son, she invited my family to her one woman show in San Francisco and invited my mother and me to Nob Hill for tea and cake. Her passion for life, her openness and her sincerity is delightful.

Edna Skinner and her friend Jean Fish were the delight of our last 50-day South America tour. Edna was the next door neighbor in the Mr. Ed television show. Her knowledge and charm were an inspiration. While having to deal with her own physical restrictions, Edna refuses to slow down. She scuba dives to be with her greatest love, the dolphin. Her courage is boundless. God be with you.

When you work on board a ship, celebrities come to you and even better, they pay you for it. I have sailed with psychic phenomenon Mr. Lubbrick, jazz greats Joe Williams and Big Band vocalist Beryl Davis, James Michener and "Up the Down Staircase" Bel Kaufman. Ship historians John Maxtone Graham, William Miller and Peter Knego, author and physical achiever Rick Hansen of 'Going the Distance-Seven Steps to Personal Change'. Gary Aldrich of 'Unlimited Access' and his lovely wife Nina, Colonel Oliver North: handsomer than as seen on television. Former Houston Rockets owner Mr. Charles Thomas and his beautiful and energetic wife Kitts, that singular sensation, Tiny Tim, the sexy Chippendales, multi-talented Terri Ralston, my love and dear close friend Gil "Zoulou" Kauhi and good 'ol Bozo the Clown, Bob Bosso, the Rockefellers, Health Crusader Patricia Bragg and the legendary actress Claudette Colbert through a communications link. I had the pleasure to meet the perfectly groomed Mary Kay Ashe, queen of cosmetics and the king of jesters and trippers, Sir Norman Wisdom. He provided clean humor, wit and charm and had the ladies vying for his attention. Celebrity's Century carried the minute Cathy Rigby and her family and the handsome Robert Conrad and his wife have been passengers on Celebrity's Galaxy. The Mercury hosted Astronaut Major General William Anders and his amazing wife, Valarie. I have the honor to know the famed chef and author of "Life is a Menu", Michel Roux and his fabulous wife, Robin. When Monsieur shares tidbits of his philosophy on the experience of food from origin to presentation, they are savored by me.

Joyce pretty much summed up the range of people we come in contact with. However, there are a few that stand out in my mind as well.

Regular paying passengers were not our only type of passengers, often we would catch stowaways. We were leaving the island of Catalina Island off the coast of the Dominican Republic when we were told there was the possibility of two uninvited guests. I was standing on the bridge prior to sailing when I noticed two men in nice clothing waving good-bye. Though often we watch passengers waving good-bye in jest, these two seemed out of place. I sent an officer down to ask them their cabin number. They couldn't say - we caught and disembarked them immediately.

This problem was a regular occurrence when we sailed to the Bahamas. Many times it was a prearranged deal of the passengers on board who had American Passports that would get off and easily fly back to the States while giving their boarding passes to illegal aliens to board and return to the States; all done for great amounts of cash. They were always caught because we had a particular security set-up at the gangway alerting us to the potential change. What that procedure was I do not say for it is confidential how we did it and I don't want to give ideas to future thinkers.

Several occasions on our way back to Miami from Cozumel, Mexico there would be Cubans floating at sea waving the ship to pick them up. By law we have to stop and rescue them. They always claimed to be out at sea for weeks at a time, however, they were not dehydrated, or even have the start of a five o'clock shadow. They learned the route of the ship calculating the time to be there when we passed, knowing we had to pick them up. This happened several times.

My wife became very upset one time when she was reading the Miami newspaper about a fourteen year old girl that had been raped and killed by a refugee that our ship had brought in the year before. It is one thing to get to freedom and another to violently abuse the system who opened their arms and allowed them in. The propaganda of the States is rich; everyone wants to attain it.

Another time we picked up refugees, the weather was turbulent. Joyce wasn't pleased knowing what happened in the past. However, passengers and crew watched as the struggle began when three inner tubes detached from each other and went in separate directions. At the same time, two of the seven men got in the water and swam towards the ship. Naturally we were upset because we had to swing the ship around several times trying to pick up each of the men on the separate tubes; the swimmers had miraculously made it. Those on the tubes were waving frantically at us to get them, they hadn't a clue that this was a 28,000 ton vessel, we couldn't just turn it around and park it next to them like a car and with difficult weather conditions. It took us nearly three hours to secure all of them. That was the last time we picked any one up and we were happy about it. Then we changed our path so as to avoid them in the future.

Another problem we had to watch for was divers along the side of the ship, often Customs was notified of a possibility that drugs were attached to the bottom of the ship and sure enough when we looked they were there. They will think of everything these people.

I was standing at the gangway in Jamaica when a nice woman in a wheelchair was taken off for sightseeing. I noticed her earlier in the cruise that she had two plastic type legs attached from both her knees. As a joke I mentioned to our Security officer, Jorge, that she probably will put drugs in them and bring them back through Customs control. We had a big laugh with this. A few hours later, two Jamaican Officers requested to board the ship to check the cabin of this woman and her traveling companion because she had been arrested while trying to deal with drugs. No words passed between Jorge and me, eye contact said it all.

One of my deck hands approached me one day to explain that he was having an affair with a passenger. I warned him of future problems and to use discretion. After a couple of days he added to the story by telling me that the woman had drugged her husband so that he could come visit her during the night. Now I told him to stop because it was too risky and stupid. That night, the husband did wake up, she started screaming that she was being attacked, and we had trouble on our hands. When everyone involved tried to explain to the husband what had been happening, of course, he didn't believe it. We had to disembark the deck hand immediately. No lawsuit was threatened; the man losing his job was enough punishment for the husband's satisfaction.

I, too, had an affair once with a female passenger when later she introduced me to her husband. I was mad because it wasn't my policy to involve myself with married women and particularly when husbands or boyfriends were there too. When she tried to make contact with me again, I explained I would not see her again. She was angry, but I had more right to be angrier. Back then the story was dropped. However, today this would not be the case. It is easy now when someone doesn't get what he/she wants, to turn against the person and create a lie to get even. Thus turning the whole story into an ugly witch hunt.

The story-wheel is continuously set in motion, never giving us a day of rest. We have those who are simply out there to have a good time filled with memories of sightseeing and shared special moments, while others are out there trying to find ways to sue, to complain or to make everyone around them miserable because they are miserable. For some, they can not leave their problems at home. They are 'supposed' to come here to clear their minds and have fun, so as to deal with their problems at home in a better light. However, some do and some don't. We are often separating spouses after a serious knock-down-drag-out fight, some physically try to kill each other and some want us to be the go between to settle their differences. One mother-in-law even wanted us to refund her cruise because her son-in-law smacked her. That isn't our business.

Thirty-seven years has shown me that situations don't change, but with the bigger ships, there are more of the same. What has changed is that we are in court more often with frivolous suits that can be settled in an orderly fashion by being just reasonable, but money talks and the ethical way of making it has somehow escaped the minds of many.

Chapter Eight
The Crew's Nest

A ship is a man's world but that world exists on a vessel called a "she". Without her there is no journey and without her being "manned" she would not sail. Without this splendid mix there would be no story.

Crew members are real people. We are not robots that are sent home when our batteries run dry; yet, when tired, we all do need a recharge. Many passengers have asked each of us what our real jobs are. Well, by now you know. Yes, for some it is a way to travel, for some a search to find themselves, for others it is better money to support their families and for still others, a career.

Now here are a few tales told out of "our" school:

We had rules to follow and officers to obey. But... Our curfew was One A.M. Often at that time we were just winding down from our long day. We would quietly (not always) get together in a staff member's cabin to have a drink and listen to music. Sometimes we would get out of control with laughter and goofing around. If caught, we received a fine and a warning. If caught again, we found ourselves on the pier, bags and all, waving to the back end of the ship.

We couldn't understand the relentless criticism of the Greek officers for everything we did - how we worked, how we talked to passengers or even our love life: nothing was right. It was their way or no way. Those of us who just let them think we were listening are the ones who kept their jobs; those who bucked them openly were simply gone. What we couldn't do was hide our actions. There was always a spy; someone always wanting to earn Brownie points. We learned quickly who they were and were on guard always.

We did some silly things to entertain ourselves: A bottle of champagne on the back deck as we crossed the equator: A "reefer" under the smoke stack to calm our nerves after being berated by an officer. A rendezvous with another crew member with one eye always open for spies.

I cried over lost loves and lost friends and lost passengers. I later laughed at the insanity of it all and decided that I would just be myself. I worked hard to respect every coworker's nationality. I worked hard to bring honor to America. I worked hard to have fun. I survived 20 years at sea with this attitude. As Johnny Mercer wrote, "You've Got to Accentuate the Positive - Eliminate The Negative..."

I was fortunate to have experienced staff members teaching me the ropes. I was already independent, outspoken and feisty - they just taught me how to use those characteristics with dignity. Maria Roubakou, Willy Feltman, Jack Dahl (Jack Eales), Paddi Parnell (Paddi Eales), Jack Freedman, Tommy VanTilburgh, Gerda (Geri) Molinaar, Lynda Smith, Maria and Dick Velasco, Yvette Petite, Kileen McNutt, Mary Larsen-Pickett, Martine Ballinger, Steve Roman, David and Rosie Lewellyn, David Lait and Brooks Aehron are just a few with whom I spent important times They spiced up daily chores, shared secret desires and fears and helped to write chapters in my life. Whether protecting each other from irate passengers or backing each other up with a story to present to an officer - we survived because we stayed together. We also laughed together.

"Skipper" was a Yorkshire terrier - a gift to the Captain from his brother. The 300-passenger vessel had just left port and the lifeboat drill was in progress. Skipper chose that moment to escape as fast as his tiny legs could carry him. The very proper Captain watched as Skipper led the drill around the decks with every officer trying and failing to catch him. He seemed to be greased. He yelped, he squirmed and he didn't stop until caught about 20 minutes later by an embarrassed officer and a perturbed Captain. We held our laughter until no one could see, then fell apart.

I was on deck announcing our horse racing event. The dancers were jockeying our wooden horses when all three started laughing uncontrollably. During the break I asked what was up. It was the wrong question. They howled even more. They couldn't get a breath to tell me. At the next break I asked them again. This time one of the girls told me to look at the man directly in front of me. I looked, then turned purple. How was I going to finish the last race now? The man was sitting in a lounge chair with a ringside seat for the races. He was enthusiastic about the sport of kings but perhaps more so for the three gorgeous jockeys. He was cradled in the chair with his legs straddling it. He was wearing a pair of shorts, but no under-shorts; his member boldly protruding in full sight. The next half hour was the most difficult that has ever passed for me. Trying to keep my composure with a microphone in hand and an audience, well... I deserve a medal. None of us could look at him for the rest of the cruise without completely breaking up.

I have had what I hope is my most embarrassing moment. A cabin stewardess could make Greek dishes, so one night she made a stew of octopus, tomatoes and onions. It was delicious and I ate heartily. Just as I was walking on stage I felt the onions dancing around my intestines. My stomach swelled to twice its size. The band was filing in on stage behind me getting into position to play some dance music. I was announcing the next day's schedule to the audience. Without any advance warning, I let out a bomb; instantaneously, the band physically fell on the floor, music sheets sprayed everywhere and their laughter drowned out my voice. The audience, naturally, looked on in puzzlement. Seeing the band in hysterics didn't help when I tried to get serious, so I explained my dilemma hoping for sympathy. The audience screamed with laughter. Twenty minutes later I had them in control enough to explain the preparations for the next day.

Another time, the ship's baker sat with me for a cup of coffee and conversation. He told me how funny I was on stage. I thought he was talking about a French show we had done but he wasn't. He asked me how the fresh bread tasted. What bread? I finally realized that I had been sleep walking. I visited the galley in pajamas, had a conversation with the baker, took the bread and left. That would explain the mystery of the crumbs in my bed. I wondered if I had walked in my sleep when no one had told me about it. It never happened again (I hope).

One night, Tommy Van was conducting the game Novelquest (an adult scavenger hunt within the room). I was behind him keeping score. The game starts by asking for a small simple item such as 'a set of black teeth' and progresses to 'two bras or two pants off the body'. As each request continues, the crowd becomes more enthusiastically involved. Once when we got to 'two pants off the body', one team leader was so excited that he took off his pants, grabbed his friend's pants and ran to the stage to present them as requested. I was on the floor in hysterics. The audience roared as never before and Tommy was speechless. The team leader was stark naked. When he calmed down and then looked down, the group roar increased tenfold. After some time, the audience got itself under control and we continued the game. It was never the same. Whether it is in the entertainment, food, bar, cabin, laundry, navigation or deck departments, everyone contributes towards having the passenger walk off having had the best time of their life. And yes, some believe that having an affair with a passenger is the best contribution they can make to the happiness of the traveler.

The crew is not always the Brady Bunch once they reach their own quarters. We had an incident so sad that I still remember it. A crew member was going to disembark the ship after two and a half years. He was leaving on Monday, but it was a holiday, so on Friday he went to the bank to withdraw his $18,000.00 savings. He neglected to leave it with the Purser for safekeeping. He went to do his duty, returned to his cabin and discovered the money had been stolen. The wrenching cry of this man should have brought the thief to his knees to beg forgiveness but it didn't. Some people were questioned but the money could not be found. Not knowing who really did it, the ship disembarked several key suspects. The man could not go home without money so he began another year's contract.

One of the night cleaners became a jewel thief. He placed the hose of his vacuum cleaner along the edges of the display windows of the boutique and sucked up the necklaces, bracelets and earrings into his vacuum. He was caught and off at the next port.

The same fate awaits the very few who have gone into the suitcases of passengers when delivering them to the cabin. Unlocked baggage is an invitation and someone will go through it, whether the airline handlers, or the longshoremen loading it. There have been a few times when a crew member's cabin was searched and items reported stolen have appeared there. The thieves are off the ship with a bad report to follow them.

I was on a ship in the Mediterranean in 1985 when TWA Flight 847 was hijacked out of Athens. We had 40 passengers going home on that flight. We were sickened at the news that someone had been murdered and the rest of the passengers were in terrible danger. I had bought a ring in Turkey for a past passenger. I knew she and her family were on that TWA flight. I gave the ring to a man from the same city as our passenger and asked him to please take it to her. He did and she wrote me about their ordeal. Her teenage son and husband were left on board after the hijackers released the women and children. Her son had to go to the bathroom and when he stood up, his tall height scared a man holding a gun and he butted him in the eye. Though he had to have several surgeries, he was all right. They were all seeing counselors and doing very well.

Next was the Egypt Air flight 648 hijacking out of Athens. I called my parents to reassure them that I would come home for vacation via the ship rather than an airplane. They agreed.

The Achille Lauro was hijacked several months later. We had Mary Kay Ashe, the founder of Mary Kay Cosmetics, on board along with 20 of her top sales producers and a full ship. As the Achille Lauro was pulling out of Egypt, we were informed by the Captain about the situation. We were not authorized to go anywhere; we were to remain at sea until further word from authorities. We sailed three days to nowhere. The bar was open and events were planned to fill the day. Extra shows were quickly put together and an intangible fear filled the ship. Several passengers wanted to helicopter off the ship, but to where? We tried to assure them that the ship had been checked thoroughly for any suspicious persons and that being in the air at that time was no guarantee of safety. We were actually safer remaining where we were.

News came that the Achille Lauro had authorization to dock in Alexandria, Egypt. The hijackers, escaping on an Egypt Air flight, were surrounded in mid air by U.S. jets, forced to land and were arrested in Italy. We heard that a passenger on board the Achille Lauro had been killed. We docked behind her at Alexandria and five of us American crew members went on board to try and lend some support. The passengers were being flown to Germany. We talked to a woman who had broken her leg when she was exiting the dining room and heard shooting. She fell down a flight of stairs and crawled into an open cabin. She explained it all started when a cabin steward had entered a cabin to clean and found four men inside cleaning guns with grenades on the bed. He ran for help, the men ran after him. One went to the bridge, one chased him and the others started rounding people up. Mr. Leon Klinghoffer, who was in a wheelchair, had been irate with the incident; unfortunately, they used him as an example. They shot him then told a crew member to throw him overboard. These men ranted to everyone that they wanted Israel to release their Shiite Muslim brothers out of an Israeli prison. Their plan had not been to hijack the ship, but to get off in Ashdod and go to the prison. Anyone in their right mind would know that there was no way they were going to get off that ship with those weapons in one of the highest security ports in the world. For those who survived the horrors on the Achille Lauro, God Bless.

My family and friends heard about the hijacking. I had already assured my parents that I was in a safe place and now this terrible news came. We couldn't get calls through and as crew, were last in line for that privilege. My Dad wasn't so worried. He told everyone to rest assured that if it was my ship, I would talk the hijackers to death and they would be running to surrender. Ha-ha Dad!

To date we have never encountered any problems of this kind. Most of the major cruise line companies continue to spend time and money to address the terrorist threat. They hire personnel from private security companies. Our company hired Israeli Security who have protected the ships for several years now without incident.

The crew need relaxation times. After all, we work seven days a week, four weeks a month and nearly eleven months a year with no day off. So we take fragments of time to relax in a mini vacation. David Lait, one of my good friends and I, enjoyed a few hours weekly. We would buy French bread, wine, cheese and pate from the island of Martinique. On Thursday nights, in David's cabin about 9:30 P.M. we would enjoy food, drink, movies and each other's company.

One Thursday we were having such fun laughing and talking that we didn't realize we were also drinking - at least not two bottles of wine and one of Sambuca. Then we suddenly looked at the movie we hadn't watched since we put it on and saw a dog Super Glued to a ceiling. For a second we thought it was on our ceiling. We couldn't stop laughing. When we realized it was the movie, we tried to rewind it to get the gist of the dog's predicament but we had to watch the movie from the beginning. It was 6:30 A.M. when the dog on the ceiling was explained and we were due at the gangway. We reported on time. Surprisingly, we were fine all day. Neither of us felt drunk until two days later, when we dropped!

Other times we would take a few hours to go to the beach, tour some of the sights and enjoy sports activities. Our recreation was sandwiched between our duties. This schedule left little time for sleep. I was afraid to miss something, so I never stopped and still haven't. There is too much to see.

Sometimes the rules were broken: a staff member having an affair with a passenger in the passenger's cabin, someone out later than curfew, or someone having an unauthorized party. At these times, the Cruise Director and I would create a plausible explanation story which we told to the Staff Captain or sometimes the Captain.

In the earlier days, punishment would either be a fine, a week's suspension on board or extra hours added to our duty. These were for a simple offense. If there was a fight involving bodily harm or a weapon, both parties were disembarked immediately. When someone pulled a prank, it generally went unpunished because the culprit usually wasn't identified.

A few pranks involved collecting little birds from ashore and putting them in the Chief Purser's desk drawer; filling an officer's bed with Jello or sending a false fax. Equally popular were greasing a door handle, making late phone calls or writing a false ship's program on April Fool's Day as well as trying to break up the person on stage. On land or sea, practical jokes are the same.

There was an unwritten law aboard that when anything transpired on the ship, it remained on the ship. Incidents were not to be reported to the office unless absolutely necessary. If you violated that law, you were disembarked shortly after for some cause or other.

I worked with a Cruise Director who truly was evil. When I came on board as his assistant, the cruise staff all handed me their resignations. I was stunned and asked them to please be patient and let me try to solve the problems. The man would scream and threaten the staff in front of passengers with the microphone on, while rarely commending anyone. He changed duties a few minutes prior to a scheduled event, making it impossible for the person to show up to run it and then writing them up.

Eventually he was caught pressuring passengers to purchase items from various stores. He was on the take from the owners. This was undermining the Port Lecturer who was paid a salary and commission for presenting maps of the stores that paid for advertisements. When the Cruise Director began to give incorrect information, passengers contacted the office directly with their displeasure. The office contacted the Captain asking what was happening on his ship. This made the Captain look uninformed. Never a good move.

The Cruise Director tried to persuade the Captain that I had framed him. I hadn't. I did discover what he was doing but I had nothing to do with the wrong he was committing. He threatened to kill me and he was capable of it. I asked Security to please follow me for all my duties on and off the ship until he was disembarked. The morning he walked off the gangway with his belongings, he bellowed that he would get me even if it took him 20 years. Thinking about him still gives me the creeps and I am always on the lookout for him.

Often times in the early days the company oversold the ship. On an airline, it's another plane. On a ship, you use the staff cabins. We were displaced to the hospital for the week or to a friend's floor. This made for party nights without censure from an officer because we had nowhere else to go to unwind. We borrowed showers; we borrowed time.

We are often asked how religion is dealt with on a ship with people of diverse beliefs. It is not a problem. Every person is free to practice their religion daily and to celebrate their special holidays and holy days without fear of reprisal.

Pakistanis work side by side with Indians; Palestinians next to Jews; Serbs next to Croatians, Yugoslavs and Albanians. There are Greeks working with Turks. These are all traditionally in conflict regarding culture and religious beliefs. They have, in common, the aim to present a united front for the pleasure of the passengers. If a rift occurs, however, it is resolved quickly before it ends in dismissals.

When we go ashore we sometimes forget what can happen there. Several of us have been mugged more than once.

My Italian friend and I walked out of New York City's main post office and got in line for a cab. A man of color hailed one for us and we took it. As I was arranging my packages, my friend, whose English was poor, asked what was being said. The man was leaning in the back seat asking for a tip. I opened my wallet to give him three dollars. Not enough. He wanted ten for himself and six for the cab driver. I told him he was crazy. All he did was wave down the cab. He pushed me away, grabbed the cash in my wallet ($500) and turned to get out. I was getting ready to hit him when I saw a large knife being held behind my friend (he didn't see it and still didn't know what was going on). I wasn't about to allow someone to be stabbed so I told him to take the money and get out. Then I climbed out of the cab and screamed for the police. Even the taxi driver froze in place. There was not one officer in sight. The Italian wanted to run after the guy but I held him back. A woman in a van appeared asking if she could help us. We tried to walk around the van to get on the street to wave down another cab but the van would move wherever we did, blocking our attempts. We started for a side street when three men of color approached us. One said he saw what happened and told me to get out of there right away. He told me that even if there was only one dollar left in my wallet, I could be killed for it. His other friend got a cab for us and pushed us into it. One of the men yelled that he was sorry and that it was a few a ------- who give the rest a bad name. We got back to the ship and I passed out!

In Ciudad Guayana in Venezuela, we were asked to put on an extra show for that night. Four of us went to the little town to buy some articles for costumes. Usually, I remove all my jewelry before going anywhere. We left in a hurry and I forgot to take off my three chains and the three small medallions attached. I was trying to manage three packages when I looked up and saw a teenager leaning against a truck. He came up to me, yanked my necklaces off cutting my neck, and ran. A man who owned a jewelry store nearby ran after the boy but couldn't catch him. He helped to wipe off the blood from my neck and we went back to the ship. I drank two shots of vodka, went to my cabin, took off my clothes to take a hot shower and the medallions fell out of my bra. I was thrilled to know the little bugger didn't get everything!

Another time I was in Miami in the crew building where we can make phone calls, purchase magazines and toiletries and post mail. I took out the tiny wallet that I now kept in my bra to pay for my postage. I thought I had returned it to its safe place but I had put it aside on top of my computer. I turned to my friend, Lynda, and said that I was almost finished. In that second my wallet was lifted. I went around the corner to buy a magazine and a juice. Then I realized my wallet was gone, yet I had my computer in hand. I ran back to where I had been. There had been two men of color behind me in line and they were now at the phone booths. I approached them asking if they had seen my wallet. Before I finished my sentence they said they hadn't seen it. Lynda and I knew they had.

I called the 800 number to cancel all my credit cards. I called my Mom asking her to inform the state driver's license bureau and the voter's registration office of the theft. As I was calling AT&T to cancel my phone credit card, the operator told me that someone was using the card and the number matched the building I was in. My friend rushed to the other booths: the two thieves were gone; the phone was hanging loose. I ran upstairs to tell the port police and give them a description of these fellows. I went back to the ship. Three hours later the Chief Electrician handed me my wallet, thinking I had dropped it. The two thieves who took my wallet gave it to him to return to me because my crew pass was also in there. The police caught up with them at the airport and filed reports against their companies. They were disembarking crew members from another ship. If stealing $200 was worth being fired, so be it but I felt violated because they were fellow crew working on ships.

Violent acts against the crew and crew against others have occurred.

One Christmas, one of our crew had about $1000.00 cash and was going shopping with a friend. On the way he was held up, taken away from his friend and shot three times in the chest. Though critically injured, he survived. Stories began to surface that it was possibly a drug deal that went wrong. Investigation showed he had an impressive amount of money in the bank but he was several years with the company and could easily have been saving it There were no drugs in his cabin; he had never been seen taking drugs or trying to sell them so the rumors stopped. He recovered from his wounds and went home.

I remember a very unpleasant incident involving a cadet crew member. He seemed to fall deeply in love with a beautiful passenger. She was married and that surprised none of us as it is a common occurrence on board. We were, however, surprised that she was responsive to the affair. Her husband was handsome and together they were a striking couple. Personally, I thought the cadet was nothing to write home about, yet he must have had something to attract such a beautiful woman and hold her interest. They took pictures together, danced together and truly seemed to enjoy being together. Although I did not see her again, it was rumored that she returned for another cruise to continue the liaison.

Several months passed. We went on vacation and returned to board another ship. I bought People magazine. I nearly fainted when I saw a photo of the cadet and the passenger he had courted. They had vacationed in Greece where he murdered her. In the interview, his father recalled that as a young boy, his son would do mean things - such as throwing the father down the stairs. I could barely hold on to the magazine. A chill spread over me and I was immediately grateful that I had never gotten to know the young man. How true is the saying that, "No matter how long you know someone you really don't know anyone". I had never come so close to a person who had committed such a heinous crime. With the introduction of the megaships, you never know where danger is lurking.

We once had a safety officer who was so vile and cruel when speaking with the crew during our lifeboat drills that one of the band members had enough. The band member grabbed a hatchet and chased the officer around the ship threatening to get him. Though he would never have followed through with it, the company took notice when others wrote to substantiate the stories about the cruelty of that officer. He was fired.

We did have a Captain in trouble by an ex-crew member who claimed he put his hand up her skirt in front of passengers. These passengers were witnesses and filed affidavits; he was then let go and sued. Times were starting to change. Rather than establishing whether the incident was a joke, a malicious act or an act of passion, it is now taken to the point of no return. What was always taken care of on board and dismissed, now ends up in court.

A sweet Filippina told me how she got her job on board. A man from the office would come to the Philippines to an agency that represented girls wanting to work on board. Much of their salary went to the agent as a finder's fee and continued on a monthly basis. Also, not only this girl, but several, told me that the representative from the office would ask them individually to come to his hotel room. Sexual favors would assure their hiring. This practice would continue whenever this person made his rounds on board to "see how the girls were doing". It took a few years but he was caught and fired because a brave girl reported him.

We had another crew member who threatened various girls of their positions if they didn't have sex with him. After four girls were fired, one girl informed me of her dilemma, fearing she was next. I referred her to the right officer on board, the matter was investigated and this person was never allowed on any of our ships again. This sweet girl is still with the company nine years after that incident.

I am woman - I am jealous. I had to get over it. Women sitting at my husband's table for dinner wanted more than dinner. Many told me their fantasies about him because they didn't know we were together. Several parents tried to marry their daughters off to him. He was good looking enough and a captain - a good catch.

I had just taken a hiatus from work when I became pregnant. I miscarried the first time but this one seemed hopeful. I was very ill and gaining weight so fast, my hormones were in overdrive. I learned that a passenger wrote a letter to my husband, now Master of the vessel, saying that she wanted to have a drink and a private conversation with him before disembarking. For the first time, my husband hid a letter from me. I called Patrizia, one of my best friends and cried on her shoulder. We searched, found and read the letter. At the formal farewell dinner she was invited to the Captain's table. I went ballistic and confronted him. He explained that he put the lady in question at his table to meet two of his friends who were single. She didn't pay attention to his friends. She eyed him all night. I wanted to claw her. She was model thin and extremely good looking. At the end of the dinner we stood in line to shake everyone's hand. When she approached me, she shook my hand, pulled me forward and said, "You are a lucky woman, believe me, if I was here another week, I would get him." I smiled and said, "That's okay, what's stopping you, you have two more days. Go for it." I winked and walked away.

After our son was born, we boarded another vessel when he was six weeks old. I was working very hard to lose the weight I had gained and what happened? Yes, another woman went for my husband; this time a crew member. She would just happen to pass our table every night when we had a drink together. She was always around. One day I overheard a conversation she had with another crew member. How could the Captain not want her with her beautiful body. The other said, "It doesn't matter, this Captain won't do it, his wife is a fantastic person, a crew member from way back and she is good looking too."

"But she is fat, why would he want her compared to me. Believe me, I will get him, it isn't hard."

I came around the door, not being able to hold back any longer and challenged her, "Listen, if you want him so badly, go for it, because if he does, then you are both trash." I walked away. I'm grateful to the one who stood up for me, but the other?

There is a very fine dividing line between the ship and the sea. I was standing on the back deck trying to organize my emotions. I took a step back from the railing and suddenly thought, only that railing divides the ship from those white foamy caps rolling from the sides of the ship. How easy it is to jump, but how similar it would be to the ship. The sea is dark, cold and lonely. The ship can be dark, cold and lonely. Many a time whether in pain or happiness, I would simply walk to the back deck. There I would sort through my thought files. There I could pull out scenes, circumstances and events that put me where I am today. At these moments, I could rationalize my life at sea.

Sea life made sense to me. I was not mature when I boarded, but within months I was. I must admit the playful side of trying to get away with something behind the officers' backs was childish, but fun. There isn't time to slow down. You don't second guess that affair, you don't second guess getting yelled at, you don't second guess your actions. Everything is full speed ahead and I love it.

Being a crew member is complex, unnerving and confusing. I have learned to sail around these shoals in my life journey. I have always stated my opinion even if it wasn't the popular one and stood up for what I feel is right. My experiences have taught me to respect more people, to look for the real reason for someone's rudeness and yet not to be afraid to protect myself.

My one regret is that I yelled at a passenger. After being on board for 14 months, I was exhausted. Not a good excuse, but a fact. She had come to me just as the band was playing my introduction to walk on stage. She wanted to be in the talent show at the last minute and wanted a prize. I snapped at her, telling her she should have come to the rehearsals and now was not the time. I did, however, eventually put her in the show and gave her the prize she wanted. She still wrote a bad comment of how rude I was and that I made her cry. Her husband wrote the same thing on another card. I was heartbroken. She was wrong in pulling me away and demanding something at the wrong time but I had made her unhappy. I don't know if she suffered from any illness or had a tragedy in her family or even if she were suicidal. I realized at that moment, I could be a cause of someone going over the edge. Also, that I was dealing with a paying passenger. That unhappy incident taught me to deal more calmly and respectfully with an unpleasant situation.

It isn't that we were so rough or mean back in the days, we just followed the rules and regulations set upon the ships to keep order among all. Some of us took that power a bit too far, it can happen, but not with all of us. I have always tried to remain firm, fair and yet try to enjoy my time as well.

Most of the time, I just didn't care what anyone else was doing, as long as the job was done and it did not hurt anyone. I'm not the jealous type so when a male crew member found a partner whether it was a passenger or crew member, it didn't bother me. However, when it involved a passenger I explained not to flaunt it, be careful of what their intentions are and don't get caught; even by me. I would have to follow the rule.

The hardest part for us is that we are looked upon as the bad guy because we enforce the procedures. If curfew is at 1A.M. and someone was out and someone complained about it, then some kind of reprimand was in order. It could be a fine, but I preferred to speak with that person and warn them that if caught again, he/she could be taken off. Parties in cabins were okay, as long as everyone was quiet, I wouldn't say much. In a way we not only navigate the ship and keep the ship clean, we had to be police keeping order. It is basically black and white, either you follow the rules or you don't. We were put in a position to be strong and keep control.

The position a person is hired for determines where and what you are allowed to do. The cruise staff, information desk, entertainers, pursers and department heads have access to the whole ship and would eat in a special section of the dining room. The other crew such as cleaners, waiters, stewards, electricians, engineers, laundry etc... would eat in the crew mess and are not allowed in public areas during their time off. (Today, this standard has changed). It is funny though, when walking around the decks how the crew would see us and cover up what they were doing or stand at attention. I guess there was a type of fear when we were seen in person, suddenly behavior was at its best. It is sort of like being the President of a little country; everyone has terrible things to say about you, but when they see you in person, they get all giddy and tongue tied.

Praise is given to all crew members from the passengers at the end of a cruise, but that praise is usually for the ones they see consistently in the public eye. The ones who never get enough credit and I highly acknowledge are the deck hands. Not only are they the helmsmen on the bridge, but when not there, they are working outside. They are cleaning the decks, painting the sides of the ship, standing at duty on the gangway to help those in need, daily washing the salty water off the ship and doing maintenance work. They work the longest hours and get the least time off all without attention or fanfare. I used to take my shirt off and work along the side of them just to help them get done faster. They are a good lot, I commend them.

Though I am a senior officer, we are neither exempt from doing goofy things nor from making mistakes. I enjoy contact sports such as basketball, volleyball and European football. I often get the officers together to play a couple of hours for the exercise of keeping fit.

One time Nina, the Casino Manager and Patrizia, the Shore Excursion Manager, organized a girl team of football to play against the men. The challenge was fun. They played hard and made us men sweat as much as they did. Nina got me however, when she ran up to me, as I was chasing the ball, lifting her blouse exposing her well-endowed breasts. In order to get even with her attempt to distract me, I ignored her. I have to admit that the girls played well, keeping us all running and made for a great game, but they lost.

113

The most asked question directed to us from the passengers concerns our private lives. Nothing substantiates better how relentless some women are even after being informed of our position in life than this next story. Though I don't get embarrassed easily, I was stunned one particular night.

I'm not sure the reason of the mystery concerning men wearing epaulets, but there is a serious force. This force causes women to think and do irrational actions. It was obvious to me that one woman was drunk the minute I was introduced by the Social Hostess to my dinner guests. I was worried walking into the dining room of where she was placed at the table. My worst fear was realized when she was directly on my right. My warning signals blew loudly in my head. Though she was accompanied by a male, she forcefully flirted from the second I sat down. After the two hours and copious amounts of wine, she became unglued. Even after I answered the passengers' questions of my personal position of being married with a son, my wife pregnant and both on board with me, that didn't seem to sway her. She kept putting her hand on my legs and inching her way to my privates. I kept putting her hand back on her own body and she would giggle every time I touched her. She didn't like the duck that was served, so she picked it up and put in on my plate.

She then placed her ultra low cut dress and large bosoms over my arm, grabbed a chocolate-dipped strawberry and took what she thought was a sensuous bite of half the strawberry. She then attempted to shove the other half in my mouth. I pulled it out and calmly thanked her and the guests for accompanying my table. The Social Hostess saw my dilemma and approached the table quickly to escort them to the show as I departed as quickly as I could physically go. I firmly informed the Hostess that in the future to be quicker in assessing a situation like that and to move the person far and away from me avoiding a scene like that again. Later I found out she was a prostitute for her male companion who was on a business trip.

I usually tell my wife of these kinds of incidents in case of false rumors starting and usually we laugh about it. She seems to let it roll off her shoulders most of the time, but there are times, I know, that she gets tired of the consistency of this kind of story.

114

Wild times are not set only with the passengers. We had a funny incident when a married high-ranking officer was dating a girl. Unknown to him she was seeing another man. But that man was of bisexual beliefs. He was seeing another man, who was also bisexual and that man was seeing another girl. So the five of them were having sex with each other without the other knowing it. How they kept this quiet without reaching the office was unbelievable. How they didn't catch anything was another feat. And how the other didn't tell about the other was phenomenal. So things can get around but at the same time never get to the right person. Now that that is said and done, on to some silly games.

Our Shore Excursion Manager from the office, David, traveled with us on the 47-day South America tour. We enjoyed playing volleyball on the court located on the funnel deck getting out our frustrations of the day. I like to play hard and mean, and I swear a lot. One time David bet me $100 that I couldn't play without opening my mouth to say something. Well, for a hundred dollars, why not. I did it - I'm still waiting for my hundred dollars - ha-ha. So in order to get David further, we hosted a table of officers in the dining room a couple of nights later. Without David knowing anything, I told the Maitre'D that it was David's birthday, even though it wasn't. The waiters came over to the table with cake singing Happy Birthday. David turned a bright red, which it is easy to make him do. He took it well, especially when passengers from another table saw who the waiters were singing to and sent over two bottles of Dom Perignon Champagne in celebration. We enjoyed our toast to the passengers and didn't have the heart to inform them of the joke.

Though I play rough in my sports, I've never really hurt anyone seriously except a few bumps and scrapes. However, I have received two black eyes within a couple of years of each other. It isn't a joke to me, but my wife gets a kick out of seeing the reaction of passengers as I walk on stage to present my officers and heads of department during the Captain's Welcome Aboard party and later walking down the corridor. Several eyes of wonder and curious gossip stirs quickly as they try to guess how the captain of the ship received a black eye.

My wife laughed hysterically when we were hosting a dinner table in the dining room when a couple complimented her on her Tanzanite collection.

She informed them that it was a very sore subject with me because it cost me a month's salary. Two hours into dinner and a couple glasses of wine, the passenger mustered the courage to ask if that is why I had my black eye. No, but Joyce sure enjoyed them trying to find the reason of the black eye.

An important factor we have to remember is that there are so many different people working on board that obviously I will run into a few I don't like or they don't like me. I try to practice that if they are doing their job, it doesn't matter. Someone should not lose their position because another has a personal conflict. I remember a time when I was Staff Captain, I wrote my report on the performance of various officers. Without my knowledge the Captain had changed my report against a man he didn't like. I found out only because someone in the office called and asked why I wrote a bad report on this guy when normally I wrote favorably towards him. I was angry that someone changed my words because of their personal differences. From that time on, I protected what I wrote.

Though I am a high-ranking officer, there are jealousies among us as well. Though I don't participate in these kinds of activities, I'm angry when someone involves me. A report was done on me concerning my physical performance. I was listed on a scale from one to ten, ten being the best, a four. I was shocked. All my physical exams were top rated; my blood work was perfect. I exercise consistently and watch what I eat. But it didn't stop the person in trying to put me down. Kind of silly, when you have been several years with a company who knows your capacity and habits. It was thrown out, I laughed it off, but I wasn't happy about the dig. I continue to do my business and that speaks for itself.

The next goofy thing we did was dangerous. My wife and I were in Cabo San Lucas and preparing to disembark the ship in California in a couple of days. My wife being from California was excited to see the Pacific Ocean. We went to the beach. Though she had a neck ache, she still wanted to go in. Our first clue not to do it was when we were standing just at the edge of the water covering our ankles when the force of the current swept my wife on her butt side. This didn't stop her. So I went first by jumping over the large wave and swimming quickly. Next she came out, but after she hurdled the wave, she came up complaining her neck hurt. I screamed for her to move fast and a thunderous wave covered her. I was in total fear of her life. I saw her twisting and turning in every direction but her head was still under water. I swam quickly, but suddenly was taken head first and slammed to the bottom. My neck crunched down and my body came over my neck. Thank goodness it was sand and not rocks at the bottom. When I surfaced I saw her dumbfounded on the beach with no suit on. She turned, saw me and called me to come in. I took my time, she didn't know I was hurt, and after ten minutes arrived on the beach. But I was bleeding from the knees and my shoulder. It scared her more than me, but neither of us believed that we were alive. That water should have killed us. She explained that she stopped counting at eleven turns and suddenly felt like God himself picked her up and slammed her down on the beach. We sat for about an hour admiring and respecting the sea for saving us, but nearly taking us too.

I don't know what to call this next incident. It is just something that happened. Probably one of those once in a lifetime experiences.

We were sailing within Canada on our way to Vancouver. We were sailing about five knots, water calm and clear skies. The pilot informed me that he saw a whale in the distance, but soon after told me it was gone. We arrived around seven in the morning, docked alongside of the pier and the safety officer called me immediately to inform me that there was a whale on the front end of the ship. The whale somehow did not get out of the way and was caught between the bulb that protrudes forward to cut through water and the front of the ship. This was not your usual whale. It was a Fin whale, the second largest known in the world. It never comes within hundreds of miles of land, let alone come inside the channel. This whale may have never seen or heard a ship in her life, therefore, she never knew what to do. But it was suspected that she was ill, for when the Canadian Coast Guard pulled the whale off, it had a horrible stench that made you sick. Though there is never a good reason for a whale losing its life, it was an asset to researchers for these whales in the sixties were put on the extinction list. Now they will soon be taken off this list for there are nearly 12,000 in the northern hemisphere and 14,000 in the southern hemisphere. There have never been any studies done on this whale because they live so far out at sea. They have been tagged over the years to enable them to be counted, but that is it. A marine biologist from the Stanley Park Marine World came to take a brain and blubber sample to be studied. *The carcass of this magnificent being was taken to a quiet cove and tied down for the sea life to feed on. After, its skeleton will go to a museum and be further studied. No one will be able to understand the hurt I felt in this incident. This mammal was about sixty meters long and approximately fifty tons, our vessel weighs in over 77,000 tons. We didn't have a chance to feel her, especially with the slow speed. Though, my two-year old son looks at it as I have caught the largest fish in the world, which excites him.*

Stories are endless for every person's life. The way of life is an individual decision. Some decisions are right and some are wrong, but these are the life's experiences.

Chapter Nine
Comparison Sailing

To experience being at sea on a cruise you need to be a passenger at sea on a cruise. No brochure promising sun filled days and moonlit nights, a neighbor's souvenir photos or rave reviews by a glib travel agent will suffice.

The essence of the experience at sea is unchanging: what has changed are the ships of today compared to those of yesterday.

The Captain and I have combined our thoughts because we have together watched the transition and are able to do the comparison. Passengers are essentially the same as they always were. Mark Twain stereotyped them many years ago and was not that far off the mark. Ships have themselves changed from elegant vehicles of the privileged classes to massive common carriers; affordable, accessible and even though "exciting and new" - impersonal.

Onboard activities are a stepping off point for comparison. Once there was enthusiastic passenger participation in each event; now, fewer events are offered and even these inspire little involvement. The daily program once appealed to a passenger's crazy side. It would tempt passengers to do things they would never do on land; ranging from the yard of beer drinking contest to men dressing as women. It required reckless abandon and the promise of no pictures. For the beer drinking contest one first had to eat two packages of saltine crackers, blow up a balloon, drink half a yard of beer, jog carefully around the pool, grab your partner and invite him/her to drink the other half. If your partner resisted, a volunteer was recruited. The winners won the grand prize of a bottle of champagne, a T-shirt and a hug from the Social Hostess. There was a consolation prize of the ship's key chain. This was advertised as a potential collector's item should the ship sink, get a new name or be scrapped.

A true highlight of the cruise was Masquerade night. It was dress-up by 6:00 PM with some passengers entering the Grand Parade and others providing a wildly enthusiastic audience. At midnight everyone took off their masks to show their identity. Cleopatra appeared one night, borne through the dining room on a elaborately decorated stretcher by eight men in loin cloths with greased back hair and decorative headbands. Others were Greeks from the first Olympics; some honored Zeus, Apollo and Athena; others would join into a harem. There were clowns, pirates, warriors, Indians, madams, dragons, can-can girls, cowboys, etc... Boundless imagination and combined talent made Masquerade Night an exciting event.

On the longer cruises of 20 days or more, the passengers were invited to dress as their favorite celebrity. Whether you were secretly a Gary Grant, Clark Gable, Marilyn Monroe, Mae West, Alfred Hitchcock or Winston Churchill, this was your night to be that person. Toga parties were added for the Roman Pompeii Romance night of ancient times.

Now in the megaship era, Masquerade balls are nearly nonexistent. Passengers are not inspired to dress up and the staff responds in kind and probably with relief. Some cruise brochures tout their absence of silly games and organized fun. Some will cheer that news while old timers will mourn it.

Horse racing used to be an afternoon at sea activity that involved big money and was an elaborate ongoing event. At the beginning of the week it was Post Time with six beautifully painted wooden horses with staff or passengers as "jockeys". The horses ran a track marked with boxes. Oversized dice were shaken in an hourglass cage; and when the dice landed, the numbers were called out to advance the horse's position. In the middle of the race, the odds were presented in a fun fashion with singing and dancing.

The ship's logo key chain was passed out for active participation, which we hyped up with the collector's item explanation. By the end of the cruise, passengers fell over each other to win this key chain. I presented one to a passenger who in turn presented me with one from the Buffalo Bills' winning of the Super Bowl. I was proud to receive it. I still have it. My husband, while an officer on board the Britanis, found a brass key chain under the carpet in his office that read, "Captains Cabin, S.S Titanic." He still has it.

Towards the end of the cruise, the horses were auctioned off. Each horse would be sold for as little as $600.00 to as much as $2,000.00. The owners would take their horse to prepare it for a popularity contest. They posted flamboyant and sometimes greatly exaggerated statistics about their mounts. They elaborately decorated their horses and paraded them throughout the ship. Whether in the dining room, show lounge or out on deck, the hype was contagious. The last night of the cruise was the big 'owner's race'. The owners formed their own cheerleading section to bet on and root for their chosen horse. The enthusiasm of the passengers rivaled that of any crowd at a racetrack.

These races are rarely seen today. On the old ships, the winning owner often walked away with as much as $7,200 to $10,000 depending on the selling price and number of bets per horse. For the staff who worked the bets and the racing event, 10-15% was taken above board. This money was used in several ways: It might be divided equally among the participating members, or if voted unanimously, it could be used for a special party or donated to a charity at an upcoming port-of-call.

Bingo is a game played then and now which is highly popular for all. Other traditional games that have survived the times are: Shuffleboard, Ping-Pong and Golf-putting. After a good round of tournament or private play, Elegant (or High) Tea and cookies and tea sandwiches is a nice way to wind down the afternoon.

Passengers enjoy visiting behind the scenes rooms and want to know about that which can not be seen. Organized Bridge Inspections (or visits) were once commonplace. Due to tightened security, these visits are now at the discretion of individual captains. Some are by his personal invitation, some upon request through the Social Hostess and some captains will not allow a bridge visit under any circumstance. Engine room visits are handled the same way at the discretion of the Chief Engineer. Galley visits are permitted and even encouraged. Passengers sign up and are informed when and where to meet for the tour.

One improvement in the bridge and engine rooms is the top-of-the-line modernization. Most of the devices are computerized with sophisticated radars, GPS (global positioning system), echosounder, fire alarms, watertight doors, fire doors, thrusters, engines, communications and safety equipment. Worldwide SOLAS (International Convention for the Safety of Life at Sea) and ISM (International Safety Management) safety regulations are implemented on board all vessels.

A fire patrolman has a much tougher job on the gargantuan vessels of today. There are fire stations throughout the ship that must be checked twenty-four hours a day. This job could take forty-five minutes on a smaller vessel. On the megaships it takes up to two hours to complete the round of one shift. This is a full time and very serious job.

With the modern detectors, a fire can be contained instantaneously with control buttons on the bridge, while the duty officer dispatches the fire squad to the exact location. They are ready at a moment's notice. The fire is contained within the boundaries of closed fire doors. In much the same way, flooding can be contained by watertight doors in the lower decks.

To satisfy tradition and superstition, there is no thirteenth deck and no cabin with thirteen on the door.

Though the technology has improved, my husband still will require that all his bridge officers know how to navigate manually. As he says, "Computers are manmade items that can break, better to be safe and know where we are at all times." He insists that his officers know how to perform skillfully and intelligently in the unlikely event of an emergency.

The type of ship and the average number of single travelers will determine what kind of Singles get-together party will be scheduled. It can be a simple informal gathering or a wild gaming party consisting of body balloon popping, picking a partner to dance and when the music stops, go and find another partner. Then musical chairs is played until two women and one man are left. The fight is on when the two women battle it out to claim him. The winners share some bubbly and invite anyone they choose to drink with them; sometimes a romance is born there. It can happen. Many former passengers have sent us invitations to their weddings.

Social gatherings for Arts & Crafts, Dance classes and organized Bridge games along with cooking lessons and hints from the Chef are activities that have never lost popularity as on board activities.

The style of dress has changed. Once, the term, "casual dress" never appeared on a program. It was requested that jacket and tie be worn to all dinners after 6:00PM and that jackets be worn for breakfast and luncheon in the dining room. Bathing suits were off limits then and now. Later, a casual night was created for a 14-day cruise while today, there can easily be three casual nights on a seven day cruise. This is due to the volume of demands by the passengers' wants and comforts. Even during the formal nights many will change after dinner into something more comfortable; sometimes jeans and tennis shoes, and then watch the show.

Theme nights were scheduled regularly to keep the interest of the passengers alive. 'Ladies Night' centered all activities on the women. The title: Miss of the vessel was awarded that night and the competition was fierce. Men and women both were dressed to the nines. The evening show featured a vocalist who sang romantic songs; there were novelty dance competitions with champagne prizes. The Cruise Director had a variety of questions to ask each contestant. Six impartial passengers were a jury to select the winner. The Miss would wear a banner for the remainder of the cruise and was bowed or curtsied to when passing her subjects in public. This night is rarely seen on board a ship today.

A large Latin group on board made for a highly charged contest. Beauty is a serious issue for them. They are very proud of their beautiful women and they should be. They will always enter the "Miss of the Ship Night" taking it quite seriously; oblivious to the light heartedness underlying the contest and its trappings. One time, a man grabbed simultaneously, the Cruise Director and me throwing us against the wall, because his 25- year old daughter was runner-up. We tried to explain that it was a fun activity, but our words fell on closed Latin ears. We were not sure whether to laugh or cry, so, we went for a drink.

We never left the men out of the festivities but they were presented much more informally. The event was usually held pool side with bathing suits as the uniform of the day. The men had to perform various feats, such as the best "Tarzan Mating Call", to take their sexiest pose, to choose the person they would like to remain with on a desert island, to confess their secret desires and to sing their favorite song. They were voted for by the 'Miss' of the ship and her five ladies in waiting.

Special ethnic theme nights were the joy of the evenings. They varied from French night-which included the Ladies Night, to Italian Bistro Night, Carnival Night and Greek Night. For the latter, we would dress in Greek style or in colors of the national flag of blue and white. Activities started with Happy Hour time with a typical drink of ouzo, Retsina wine or strong Metaxas brandy. The menu included dolmades (grape leaves with rice and meat), grilled squid (kalamari), tzaziki sauce (garlic and yogurt), eggplant dip, fried zucchini, feta cheese, saganaki (fried cheese) Greek salad and bread. Dinner was moussaka (eggplant, meat and potato casserole), pastichio (noodles, meat and cream casserole), roasted lamb and grilled chicken with lemon potatoes. The deserts were baklava (filo dough with nuts and syrup), galaktobouriko (custard in filo dough) and Greek coffee. Everyone then went to the show lounge for a show presented by the Greek Choir. The members varied from cruise to cruise, depending on their talent and ignoring their rank. Hostesses were enlisted to complement the folk dances. The famous dances included: the Kalamatianos - the National dance of Greece; the Yerakina -a dance from Thessaly - which portrays the meeting of village boys and girls as they express their desire to get to know each other better. The familiar Zorba's dance, the Syrtaki, was performed with eight simple steps, with more difficult ones to be added later. Many dances were performed in the costume typical to the region where the dance originated. The choir and the bouzouki (a guitar type instrument) always produced a happy audience brimming with vigor, fun and passion.

Though all nationalities of crew members take care of the passengers with 100% devotion and pride, the all-Greek crews were exceptional. They would go the extra mile or two, even while off duty to fulfill the needs of their passengers. Their memories for detail were flawless. They would remember you and what you liked when you became a repeat passenger. In addition, the ship's cleanliness is noteworthy on a ship run by Greeks. This is part of their tradition. It is true that the streets are often littered but inside the Greek house, it is immaculate. To staff a ship exclusively of Greeks is too expensive. Profit makes the world go around, the world go around... Staffing a ship with multi-nationals draws a variety of clientele. When traveling on a vessel run by Italians, you will have that special pasta with their famous sauces; or with the French, their fine wine and special cheeses but the style of 'one' nationality remains limited to a handful of ships.

The word "smoking" immediately divides people into opposite camps. They become more volatile than when they discuss politics or religion. There were, on the older ships, smoking rooms. Today, smokers inherit the port or left side of the vessel. However, smoking is permitted at the bars and should a bar be located on the non-smoking, or starboard side, it precludes the non-smoker from sitting there in comfort. There are ships that are completely nonsmoking vessels and booking them to capacity does not present a problem. I have often had to ask a smoker to extinguish a cigarette or cigar while the show is in progress because of the performers. Many times the passenger has blown a huge puff of smoke in my face in response. They proclaim that they paid for the cruise including my salary and will do as they please.

Having the separate rooms was a good way to keep all concerned happy. Newer vessels today build cigar rooms to satisfy all passengers' wishes. There are always those who will chomp on a lighted cigar and parade around with it. Now, peer pressure is great enough to discourage the culprit, thus taking away the task of a staff member who may easily be ignored.

Passengers used to have the advantage of an up close and personal feeling when a 'Celebrity guest' was on board. Today, these guests usually come when a particular group traveling has requested them and only those in the group will have the chance to spend time with them. Though the person is in the public eye, he or she will not do anything more than sign an autograph. A good example from the up close and personal days was the famous Mr. Blackwell who came on board with his friend, Robert Spencer. A great team. Mr. Blackwell was an adopted Godfather for one of our great entertainers, Mr. Leslie Jon. Through Leslie, Mr. Blackwell would bring his designs and have us staff members do a fashion show for the passengers. When I was asked to come to his cabin, I was not thrilled. I never saw myself as the model type. I was too athletic and I had muscles from swimming. Waif-like, I wasn't. I walked in and Mr. Blackwell looked at me and said, "Oh, no, she won't do, she is much too fat." I was stunned and walked out. Mr. Spencer came after me and asked me to please wait a minute; he claimed to see something good under the fat cells.

For the next two hours I tried on outfits and spike heeled shoes. At one point, Spencer had me try on a formal blue sequined dress that looked as if it were made for Princess Diana. It was far too long. He told me that the models were usually five feet eleven inches and above. I am five foot six and a half inches. "No problem", Spencer just took a pair of scissors and chopped off the excess. Ouch! I then asked, "Spence, how much is this dress worth that you so nonchalantly discard?" "Oh, about $10,000.00." "Ah", I screamed, holding out my arms to air my armpits, "I'm sorry but I'm sweating in it." Spencer laughed. He knew I was nervous and my shyness was a welcome relief from the professional models he usually handled. I was then sent to the Beauty Salon for a make up and hairdo and told to report later for the show.

I wasn't pleased at the thought of facing Blackwell again. He didn't see me until he called my name from the stage. When I came out, he was tongue-tied. As I passed him I whispered, "What is the matter? Someone finally get you to hush up!" I sauntered past him and on to the stage where I received the loudest ovation. I modeled four dresses and gowns: I felt nice. Blackwell held my hand asking the audience if I wasn't what everyone wanted to be. I gave him the "fish eye" to remind him that he originally had rejected me as a model. It was fun and meeting Blackwell was a positive treat. He did give the other girls a souvenir dress and promised to send me mine. I am still waiting.

The devotion of repeat passengers has decreased steadily over the years. The repeat percentage often ranged as high as 90, while today an average repeat percentage is approximately 40. This decrease is in large part due to the increased size of the vessel and the resultant loss of a family atmosphere. The repeat passenger knew he or she was returning to a shipload of the same crew members. Today, contracts range from four to seven months and the crew member is rotated among seven to twenty ships in a fleet. When passengers repeat with a cruise line now, seeing a familiar face among the crew is a bonus. They re-book for the security of the food presentation and quality, cleanliness and safety they previously experienced. There are some, however, who are so devoted to their favorite crew member they will make certain that person is on board before they book a cruise. We have had many couples traveling with us even today who have followed us from ship to ship and even company to company. We are grateful for their intense loyalty and try never to disappoint them.

One game was banned on most ships by nervous companies, living in fear of offending or worse still, being sued. In question was Novelquest billed as the adult scavenger hunt without leaving the room. Though there was never a complaint from anyone, off it went. It was always described before the game began that it could get wild and for those who did not want to participate or might feel offended, they might be happier elsewhere.

Prior to playing Novelquest, we as staff put on a skit that is rarely performed today, to the dismay of many repeat passengers who took pleasure in it. It was called, "If I Were Not Upon The Sea." This skit consisted of about eight members of various departmental staff who dressed in an exaggerated version of an everyday job. We came out individually singing what we would be fictitiously doing if not upon the sea while continuously forming and reforming a line. The comical part was what each person did to the next person after they sang their part. For example: the first person would sing -

> "If I were not upon the sea
> Something else I'd rather be.
> If I were not upon the sea,
> A blackjack dealer I would be.
> "Hit me once, hit me twice,
> Twenty-one or bust."

The singer wore a croupier's outfit but with exceptionally large bosoms. The next performer would sing his part and then while singing, reach over and pop the water balloon bosoms any time during the act. All down the line, each individual would do something crazy to the persons on each side of them. The finale would be the cruise director coming out in a tutu wanting to be a ballerina. By this time in the cruise, all the passengers knew who each crew member was so they could personally relate to them on stage. The cruise director had a surprise waiting under his tutu while the person next to him had something up her sleeve as well. We continued this skit on and off the stage, by pulling weekly pranks on each other. One time I was a seamstress and would be after the undertaker next to me. He put a basket in his pants so when I went to grab his privates, I hurt my hand. I then turned to the cruise director, and with my oversized scissors, proceeded to cut off his privates. This caused an uproar in the audience. Without missing a beat, we proceeded directly into our next game, which was Novelquest. At this time it was easy to get even with the undertaker, who was keeping score for the game. At the last minute, we made one of the quests a discovery of what was in the undertaker's pants. Twenty-five groups of people tried ripping his pants open. Yes, by all means, this is total silliness, but made for good times.

The "If I Were Not Upon The Sea" skit was originated in England in the Holiday camps during World War II. After the war, many of those who worked the camps came on board as Cruise Directors. What they did then in the camps, they introduced on board as entertainment schemes. The passengers received it well and looked forward to seeing the announcement in their daily programs. The entire style of entertainment and related activities is in the hands of the Cruise Director and the cruise line.

At one time, both the day and night activities were centered on a theme. As staff, we stayed with the theme and performed in the show at night with just four dancers, two singers and a comedian. One or two entertainers were scheduled for interim nights. Entertainment shows on today's ships still have two or three guest singers, comedians and variety acts who stay on board a few weeks at a time. The production shows are staged by professional companies who remain on board for several months at a time. Up to 30 members perform two or three shows a week which are staged in Las Vegas style. The modern day emphasis is on food as a theme and frequently carries through to the midnight buffets. There are, for example, Country Western Night and Tropical Night for which you can wear outfits to match the theme for the midnight country barbecue or the fruits of paradise presentation.

Various trivia games are organized between shows and with the popularity of karaoke from the bars and restaurants on land, it is now an onboard activity.

Some pool side games have been taken out of production such as the famed 'Yard of Beer Drinking Contest', as mentioned before. The reason it has been taken out again is fear of a lawsuit and the very few who have mentioned that they feel it promotes alcoholism. Alcoholism was _never_ the intent, it was again something brought on after the war and used as a tension breaker. Every staff member wants desperately for the passenger to have a vacation and enjoy a good laugh. So if one activity has brought pleasure to a number of passengers and not to others, it is hoped the next day's program will appeal to another group. There is something for everyone and a ship's complement is geared to make this happen.

Over time everything changes. The mores of the day are naturally brought on board by the passengers. The smoking, alcohol vs. alcoholism, and the concern for the environment; specifically, waste disposal methods are current concerns. The cruise lines have recognized these concerns and have addressed them vigorously. The large ships are scientific wonders; able to burn garbage in incinerators, recycle glass cans, packing materials and paper and to purify wastewater into clear water that can be used in the laundry. They are environmentally conscious even to the type of exhaust that is put out in the air. The new smaller ships are also implementing these programs.

During the Captain's Welcome Aboard party, the photographer used to take a picture of each person shaking hands with the captain entering the party. Today, this tradition has been set aside on the larger vessels due to the volume of people and the numerous camera flashes directed at the Captain. Individuals who would like a picture are always accommodated upon request.

Captains' dinner tables have changed over the years. A handful of ships today do hold to the tradition of sitting the same people at his table throughout the cruise, irrespective of its length. If the Captain were unavailable, another officer took his place. Now, between the Captain and his officers they invite a variety of people to dine on special nights. The Hotel Manager, Staff Captain, Assistant Hotel Manager, Guest Relations Manager, Doctor, Chief Engineer are the usual hosts.

Being selected for this honor is multifaceted: A VIP list from the head office, a personal relationship with the officer hosting the table, a recommendation from the Social Hostess, or a multi repeater with the Line. You can also be chosen by being in the right place at the right time.

The Captains were once the highest paid personnel on the ship, as well as the most respected. Special staff members are now paid more. Where once a staff member might perform three to five distinct jobs, the larger ships hire personnel to fill each of those positions.

Cruise ships have grown in capacity from 180 to 1200 passengers - to 2100 to 3700 passengers at a time. The Captain's responsibility has grown in quantum leaps. From handling a 3,500 to 28,000 ton vessel-now to 48,000 to 142,000 ton vessels are under his command, with the concomitant increase in crew. The modern ships are comparable to a city put to sea. The older ships can not be rebuilt because of the building materials used. It is far cheaper to start from scratch and build. Today a ship is worth $350 million dollars or more not including artwork, equipment and necessities. The increasing liability and accountability on the Captains' shoulders to man large floating hotels has not increased their power. The payment has not escalated in kind. It is comparable to the police and firefighters who risk their lives to save others. As the population they are expected to serve increases, their salaries do not. It is the same on board the megaships.

Today a Captain can walk around the ship and many crew, as well as passengers can not identify him. Often I am sitting with my husband when someone greets him saying, "Hello, Doctor." This is understandable. In 1988 several companies changed policy and permitted epaulets to be worn by personnel who formerly did not qualify for this honor. This was once reserved for the navigational bridge officers, engineers and electricians who worked hard to pass the stringent requirements involved to earn their certificate. The cumulative amount of education from the navigation and engine departments to the added crew wearing these epaulets is impressive. In a land-based society, democracy is to be desired. On board ship, there is a hierarchy and that system works for all concerned.

Many times passengers write comments identifying as an officer, one who was not and because of mistaken identity is subject to false accusations. Often it is just written that an officer did something or other and without more specific information, the comment ends with the comment sheet.

There are new titles and positions. The Chief Purser was once in charge of the cabins and the monies on board. Now that position is listed as Assistant Hotel Manager and a new position of Hotel Manager was created to supervise all those in the hotel department. The Information Desk is now called the Guest Relations Desk with Guest Relations Officers, including a Guest Relations Manager, which is a new position and was once one of the duties for Chief Purser.

Several titles that have changed are: The Maitre'D - now called the Restaurant Manager along with his Assistants, the Chief Steward - now called Chief Housekeeper along with his Assistants, some Cabin Attendants have the title of Butler and service the suites and penthouse suites exclusively. Stewards are now Attendants. The title of Social Hostess still exists along with two or three regular hostesses but there are additional positions of Entertainment Hostess, European Hostess and even Society Hostess. Once the hosts and hostesses were responsible for handling sound, lights and props for the shows; now, there is a Production Manager with all full staff and a Broadcasting Manager with staff. For the Deck Department there is now an Environmental Officer. To note, some companies do not use the word Assistant for the second in line but use the word 'Deputy' instead.

A Cruise Director's position today has less responsibility than previously. The current position can be likened to that of a Master of Ceremonies and supervisor of the staff. In the past, he or she would create the daily program, put a show together, perform one or two shows, make up games, tell wild stories and be the liaison between crew and officers. Along with this lesser responsibility, the style of a Cruise Director has altered. As our current older directors resign, their personalities; the spontaneity, the quick wit and secure self image leave the gangway with them. Their experiences in meeting different people and traveling to various ports made them global citizens. Their personalities, unencumbered by fear of being politically incorrect, made them who they were. Their modern day replacements are business like, practice being non-offensive to any passenger (which is impossible) and are classroom or video trained. A few Cruise Directors do have an advantage when they follow in the footsteps of their parents who gave them a start by raising them around the ship life or they have a natural instinct.

So it is easy to find the good and bad with the old and the new. It is left to each person's personal preference in the desire to enjoy the cruising journey. The older and experienced know two styles of cruising, while the younger and inexperienced learn just the one style. There is no right and wrong, it is just time sailing on.

So for those first time cruisers or for those who have not noticed the rank and file order of the ship, the following lists explains who is who on board. Greeting an officer by his correct title will show him respect and you just might end up at a table he is hosting.

Here is the ranking of stripes, the title of that rank along with the color signifying the department.

The ultimate official of the ship is The Master Captain who wears the Commodore's Bar with Braided Gold Stripes on black. There can be more than one captain, but only one Master. Listed are the following ranks:

4 Gold Stripes:
Staff Captain gold on black, Chief Engineer gold on purple, Hotel Manager gold on white.

3-1/2 Gold Stripes:
Chief Radio Officer on green, Staff Engineer on purple, Chief Electrician gold on burgundy, Asst. Hotel Manager/Chief Purser on white, Senior Doctor on red, Cruise Director on status[1], Food Manager and Bar Manager on sky blue.

3 Gold Stripes:
Chief Officer on black, First Radio Officer on green, Second Engineer on purple, Electronic Engineer and A/C Engineer on burgundy, First Purser on White, Doctor on red halves, Restaurant Manager stars on black, Executive Chef on Status, Chief Housekeeper silver straight stripes on white, Guest Relations Manager straight halves on white and Casino Manager straight stripes on white.

2-1/2 Gold Stripes:
Assistant Cruise Director on status , Assistant Casino Manager straight on white.

2 Gold Stripes:
Second Officer on black, Security Officer straight halves on black, Third Engineer and Amos Controller on purple, Second Electrician and Second Electronic Engineer on burgundy, Second Purser on white, Nurse on red halves, Social Hostess on status, Asst. Food Manager/Provision Master on sky blue, Asst. Restaurant Manager stars on black, Sous Chef/Pastry Chef on status, Asst. Bar Manager on sky blue, Asst. Chief

Housekeeper silver straight halves on white, European Hostess and Guest Relations Officer straight halves on white, Program Coordinator, Onboard Sales Coordinator and Printer are straight stripes on white and Team Activities Coordinator on status.

[1] Gold Stripe:
Apprentice Deck Officer on black, Apprentice Engineer on purple, Apprentice Purser on white and Computer Operator on status.

These Officers' Insignias mean nothing to many people and everything to many others. Those who have served in the military or on ships know how hard it is to earn the respect and to gain the knowledge it takes to add those prideful stripes to their shoulders. Taking a minute to acquaint oneself with this protocol can make you a step closer to the life on board ship and provide a free course of study.

[1] *'On status' does not refer here to a color, but to the fact that these positions carry the 'equivalent rank' of a uniformed member of the crew.*

The Engine Room colors of purple and burgundy are worn to honor and respect those crew who lost their lives at sea on the Titanic.

Some advancements have made life on board easier. Though we still have a telephone operator, they are no longer needed to connect us to other parts of the ship; we can dial directly. The operators are available for information, emergencies and assistance.

While pressing rooms were once in vogue, now there is full laundry service that does it for you. Though Bootblack service is not directly available, your cabin steward or butler will be of assistance.

Elizabeth Arden was once the popular Beauty Salon on board along with a Barber service, it is all now combined under the Steiner Company which includes a complete highly chic and fashionable spa with amenities that rival the finest on land. Aerobics, toning and gym equipment are all supervised by a certified staff.

The shops and boutiques on board along with the photography department have not changed except in size and a variety of offerings.

The most recent addition to the concessions on board is the art auctions. A professionally trained Art Auctioneer is there to auction works of Salvador Dali, Krasnyanky, Pablo Picasso, Marc Chagall, Tarkay and many others. A good chance to learn about Art at your leisure.

Some changes have been for the better. The unusual incident of a high-ranking officer abusing his girlfriend while working on board now results in his immediate dismissal. In the bad old days, the occurrence would have been swept under the ship and rolled out with the current. With the new laws and more companies listed on the stock market, minute incidents stand to be investigated and are followed by a reprimand of sorts. The institution of safe deposit boxes in the individual staterooms is more convenient and extremely safe.

Another modern improvement concerns the larger and more private facilities for the crew. Before there was the basic crew and officer mess, now, there are officer, staff and crew messes, along with a specialty mess satisfying the food requirements of the Indonesians - because there is such a large number of them on board. There is now a crew gym, bar, pool, library, gathering room, and a Team Activities Coordinator. This person directs activities involving crew in: sports tournaments with other ships, cleaning beaches of various islands and ports-of-call, raising money for charities and donating toys, clothes and such for the less fortunate. There are language lessons provided by volunteers, party and movie nights. There are various monetary and certificate awards for outstanding performances in service to passengers along with their treatment of fellow crew members. At one time if one did a wrong deed, they were simply dismissed. Now there is a verbal warning, then three written warnings, a meeting with the Captain, then a dismissal. If, after all this, the mistakes persist - oh, well.

The types of passengers so eloquently described by Mark Twain in The Innocent Abroad, have not changed. He recalls carving his own initials into the railing of an outside deck as an officer watched. Today, passengers still engage in the sport of carving: all over the elevator doors and the hardwood cabinets of the library. The "art" of graffiti decorates the stateroom walls. Even the ships' art displays are not sacred. Statues and paintings are damaged or stolen on the theory that purchase of a cruise ticket allows theft.

Comparisons prompt discussion. We, who have lived our lives at sea, have watched the mystique of a cruise disappear and the safety of a vessel take on sophistication. We have progressed from Mayflower to Megaship. But the sea remains as landlady.

Chapter Ten
Thanks for Your Memories

The rhythm of the waves at sea is seductive. It inspires a passion and an energy and people are always changed by it. Seldom does a personality change, however. If a passenger or crew member boards with a positive attitude; the result will be a joyous educational experience. If a passenger or crew member boards looking for trouble, they will find it because they generate negative feedback. Some will board without expectations and these are the easiest to please.

Whether coming on board for a vacation or embarking on a new life experience, you are different when walking off. It may have been the best or the worst cruise you booked. For the passengers' sake, the crew will always try their very best to create an atmosphere of respect, fun and sometimes fantasy. Their positive attitude can make that effort a pleasure instead of a drudgery.

When we travel, there is always the unexpected pleasure and the unexpected problem. I feel that the best advice is to just get out there, enjoy the best way you can with an uncensored-open mind. Ralph Waldo Emerson once said, "Though we travel the world over to find the beautiful, we must carry it with us or we find it not."

Very few past passengers still have the souvenirs of their cruise - The photos of the table mates with waiter standing behind, daily quizzes, business cards and the ship's daily program are seldom saved. But we have saved their gifts to us.

Thanks for your memories. Thanks to each passenger who used time and talent to write their thoughts in words and music, poetry and prose. We remain on board; with only tiny segments of time to absorb your leaving us, when another shipload of you arrives. Yet, when we have souvenirs of you and know that you cared that we cared about you, it is a comfort and joy for us. Here are only a few of the memories you have given us.

Written in a rush on May 19, 1985 by C.A. Bausback traveling on the Stella Maris Antiquity cruise while sailing between Delos and Paros:

"THE STELLA MARIS MADRIGAL

I had planned my whole vacation
When I got the Sun Line News
That the Stella Maris Two
Would go on a Gala Cruise
So I sent off my deposit
In the early morning mail
And then I started waiting
For the Day that we'd set sail.

On the afternoon we boarded
All our hearts were light and free
We were the greatest people
Who had ever put to sea
Once we'd stored our luggage
Put away the odds and ends
Then we mingled with each other
And we soon were all fast friends.

On the dear old Stella Maris
Is a grand hotel afloat
But that broken down piano
Makes the only sour note
Much better we should listen
To some music that is canned
But the one redeeming feature
Is the Stella Maris Band.

And the crew is always scrubbing
Every square inch of the boat
So I'm sure the Stella Maris
Is the cleanest ship afloat
Now if I lose the tune here
And I don't know where I'm at
Then please just give me your key
And I'll sing it in your flat.
At the top of each days schedule
They give us words to speak
If you'll memorize them carefully

You'll soon absorba da Greek
All the stewards in the restaurant
Always know just what to do
Everyone time you order one egg
They will always bring you two.

Babis-Kostas-Nikos-Lefteris
And Panagiotis too
Maraskevas and Vagelis
Theadoros one and two
Ilias-Aris-Ioannis
Boy my tongue is getting twisted
And there are so many more
That I haven't even listed.

Both dear Nota and Sweet Vanna
Make the shore excursions hum
Just show them a slab of marble
And they'll know what age it's from
We've walked through many fallen cities
where the voice of history speaks
and the ruins are so terrific
No one builds them like the Greeks.

We saw old men riding donkeys
And children planting plants
And women in the cities
Wearing baggy Turkish pants
There was one rare golden moment
No one else has ever had
We stood in the ruins of Troy
And listened to the Iliad.

And our Dear Professor Adronikos
Found some gold and bones and leather
He said, "This must be Alexander."
So he glued him back together
Then there's Julie in the Gift Shop
Selling memories of our trip
And all her wares are tagged with

The cheapest Prices on the ship.
Willy Feltman is our MC
He's a most amusing guy
He can always keep us laughing
And he doesn't even try
He's also a ventriloquist
Which is really rather silly
'cause he keeps a puppet in a box
That has a better voice than Willy.

When Joyce mans the colored spotlight
She can go from white to puce
All the dancers come out red or blue
While the singers are chartreuse
But Joyce has other talents
Hidden in her bag of tricks
For she won two swimming races
In the Junior Olympics of seventy-six.

And the smile of Little Carmen
Has now captured all the barmen
All the near men and the far men
cigarette men and cigar men
And when Carmen does the fado
Or the fast Zapateado
With her heels in high staccato
We envy Santiago his tomato.

When we dance to Mitch's music
Why it really is a treat
For the melody is Mitch's
But the side man makes the beat
Tony Chrissos has a great voice
That is headier than wine
And his version of "Kalinka"
Sends the goose bumps up your spine.

The guitar is strummed by David
As he lifts his voice in song
With melodies so lovely

You can't help but sing along
And then Mari Anne comes slinking
Dressed in black just like a cat
And the cat plays Swedish polkas
Now what do you think of that?

And of course there is Jack Freedman
And his brother the Great Star
He plays a broken down piano
In the Old Cairo Bazaar.

And everybody loves our Lena
The Sun Lines Mother Hen
If I knew we could have Lena
I would take the cruise again.

Tomorrow morning I will stand there
As forlorn as I can Be
With my luggage all around me
While my heart is out at sea
Yes, they call this cruise a Gala
It's a word that's pretty cool
But it's more than just a Gala
It's the SUN LINES CROWNING JEWEL."

This one was written on 8/10/86 on board the Stella Oceanis in Greece. These verses were written to the tune of "Thanks for the Memories". To the unknown author, 'your thoughts are forever engraved for all to read':

"Thanks for the memories
Of seven days in Greece
On Stella Oceanis
Of Istanbul
And bellies full
Must this cruise ever cease?
Let's change course tonight

Thanks for the memories
Of donkeys climbing high
To heights men rarely try
With us on top

140

They dip and clop
To castles in the sky
How scary it was.

Now that we're nearing
Piraeus
We don't want to say
Kali spera
Yet soon we must say
Kali mera
You can't learn Greek
In just a week.

And thanks for the memories
Of dolphins on parade
The widow's masquerade
No Mykonos
Instead of Samos
The Turkish deals we made
What bargains they were.

Thanks for the memories
The meals par excellence
That tricky Grecian dance
Acrop-o-lis
The beach top-less
Les femmes jolie de France
How splendid they were.

Pity our fellow Americans
What's come of their
pioneer spirit?
Poor Europe, they
won't venture near it
Let's pray this fear
Won't last all year.

Now -thanks...
for the quality
Of being from the start

A crew of boundless
heart
You've given so
We hate to go and
'from these decks depart
We thank you so much!!!"

On board the Stella Solaris in 1987, Dale Zachery wrote these
fine words of prayer:

"I don't mind the rough seas
I don't fear the gale and storm
I don't hate the strong winds
I don't flee the lighting and thunder

All I ask, God, is a strong vessel

One that is of steel and rivets
One that is a refuge and home
One that will keep me afloat
In the midst of all of life's weather

She doesn't have to be beautiful
She doesn't have to be young
Just my hope for a good life
on the waters of the world

That move me from port to port
In your world so diverse and beautiful
And yet so frightening
Because of its dimensions

All I ask,

All I ask, Father, is a strong vessel
To keep me safe
And I'll follow wherever your winds
lead.
Amen."

This poem was on board the SS Britanis some time between
1990 and 1992 by Lillian Burak with her sentiments of:

"LIFE CAN BE BEAUTIFUL

Britanis is a ship,
That's really great,
I find it's the best,
In all the state,
The crew is here, to try and please you,
They graciously do what ever you ask them to do.
The food is great, your palate it will tease,
Forget the calories, eat what you please.
If you're lucky, you just might have a date,
And maybe they'll turn out to be your mate.
And if you're married, you know what you can do.
Hugging your mate, and say "I Love You".
You will be filled with joy and surprise,
When you see the love in their eyes.
So after all is said and done,
Britanis is the best ship, to have fun."

Here the poet tries to capture the Captain's thoughts as he guides
the vessel through the seas. This was on board the Victoria on February 18,
1990 by Mr. Selby:

"Our Captain on the Victoria has just cleared the Harbor for the
open sea,
    And on his mind as he stands on the bridge,
    His thoughts of the loveable sea.
    The sea, the sea, the open sea.
    The blue, the fresh, the ever free.
    Without a mark, without a bound, it runneth the Earths wide
region round.
    I'm on the sea, I'm on the sea, I am where I shall ever be.
    With the blue above, and the blue below, as the Victoria ship
cruises smoothly on the sea.
    It plays with the clouds, and marks the sky, and like a cradle-creature
lies.
    I'm on the sea, I'm on the sea, I am where I shall ever be.
    With the blue above, and the blue below, sailing the Victoria as
we go."

Upon our exploration of South America two wonderful gentlemen collaborated on the following: Words by Mr. Phil Morrison and music by Mr. Gary Lawrence on 10/3/90 on board the SS Britanis:

"A SOUTH AMERICAN CRUISE

Dancing waves to Natures Tune
The lofty Sun is high at noon
Distant Clouds deceive the eye
Soft White Shapes drifting by

As the wind Plays Melodies
Above the open seas
Islands of your mind
The Creator's Grand design

Majestic Mountains Standing tall
Crowned in white - Dressed for us all
Cruising through the Narrow Straits
Allowed to Pass through nature's gate

You can almost hear them say
"Magellan Passed this Way"
With Great anticipation
To reach our destination

Close now - we hear the roar
Two Oceans meet as if at war
Gradually the winds die down
Alas: There's something new we've found

The winds cry out to warn
The Battlefield - Cape Horn:
We continue to move forth
Our direction now is North

On to Buenos Aires Now
As one ship met another's bow
One man almost blew his top
Made no difference

At least that's what we thought
So now they've closed that port
Because we couldn't go
Our next stop-was Montevideo

A South American Cruise
Chile and Argentina
A South American Cruise
Dancing Brazilian Samba

Where tropical breezes blow
Their mountains capped with snow
That's where I want to be
Living this Fantasy

Following is a letter written when a man who traveled with us read the literature recounting the history of the S.S. Britanis. He realized that the ship he was now standing on was once involved in a history he witnessed many years before. Thank you to Mr. Art Sulzer, Room 406, on 9/7/94. You are commended for your duty during the war and for acknowledging the history of a grand Lady.

"Your article on the Britanis brought back memories, I was in that convoy of November 1943. I was 3rd Engineer aboard the U.S.Army Transport Thomas H. Barry Sistership of the Morro Castle which burned off Asbury Park 1936. We were attacked by German Torpedo planes. A large Dutch Liner Manix'Van Oldenbact was sunk. The Grace Liner Santa Elena received a torpedo in her aft alley. Troops were removed at sea. The Santa Elena was being towed into Phillipeville, Algieria by a tug. She was about 100 yards from shore and from our ship. Suddenly she started to sink rapidly by the stern. We could see the few remaining crew members jumping off the starboard bridge wing. Then she went down.

The Germans reported a heavy loss of troop ships 10-12. What happened during the night the ships went into Algiers, Phillipeville, & other ports, hence in the morning the German planes found fewer ships that were continuing on. Note the (4) Matson Liners were in many convoys with us. In very heavy weather due to their speed and sea keeping ability, there were released from convoy and just took off."

145

This offering was by Mr. Rod Senn, who was one of our lecturers from the last 55-day South America Cruise of 1994. He wrote these humorous limericks to recognize some unforgettable passengers as well as the Captain of the vessel:

A Captain named Korres, A Greek.
Had a ship that was old, but unique.
His sailing was great
Til he went up the Plate
And he said, "We're too far up the creek."

Now Annie and Ada and Hugh.
Please bid old Britanis adieu
You drove us all frantic
With every new antic.
Signed: Passengers, Staff and Crew.

These are only some of the passengers' gifts to us. The sea has a way of inspiring people to deeper than surface emotions which they feel free to express. We as staff encouraged that and rejoiced in it.

Tears were not unusual when the disembarkation announcement was heard. Hugs were plentiful. Wishes for a safe journey home were ceaseless as well as promises to keep in touch. I lived up to that promise as much as I physically could. Over the years, I have shared the grief of a passing of a favorite passenger with families who were kind enough to inform me of it. This too, is a practice and a nicety that is diminishing and will probably disappear shortly.

I became very attached to a three-year old girl, Suzi Graham, whose mother was a few months pregnant. I was totally charmed by the child and showered her with constant attention. She responded to it and was a delight. She cried as she walked down the gangway. This brought tears to the staff and me and some passengers who saw her leave. She slowly crept around the corner until her little blond head was gone. I corresponded with the family for almost three years. Suzi and I shared the thrill of the birth of her brother, her new life experiences and her joys. Then they moved, my letter was returned and I never heard from her again. It broke my heart. I only hope all is well with the family and that they are happy and in good health.

Another young girl of about eleven or twelve years old, named Laura Breitzman, came aboard with us on the Antiquity cruise with her grandparents. I adored her. We traveled ancient sites together and shared new experiences. It was a thrill of a lifetime for her and such fun enjoying the time with her grandparents. Over time, I got to know her mother through our letters. We wrote each other for about thirteen years concerning Laura and her activities. Then one day, contact was lost. It was another difficult time for me, because I so enjoyed her spirit and her coming of age. Good thoughts go to you and your family as well.

I pay tribute to those passengers who made my days so enjoyable. Time has taken them away from their families and from me: Colonel Federico his wife Betty, Schael, Sally Richmond, Duchess Smith, Colonel and Mrs. Millson, Mr. Bob Seidenberg, Ann Henkins and most of all Jules Madere. I knew him for twenty-five years and he came on a cruise to meet my husband and my son. Our time together was brilliant. Cruising was a first for him and he embraced it with open arms. He had booked another cruise and had to cancel when he was told he had cancer five days before the sailing. Both our hearts were broken. I never saw him again. I sent him the Totem pole from Alaska that he wanted, along with books to read. I spoke with him every week on the telephone. The inevitable time came when I could not reach him and shortly after his daughter Marsha called me with the news of his passing. Staying in touch with Marsha and her mother, Lillian, is a comfort and keeps his memory alive. Jules, I know you are there; you will never leave my side.

Oops!

We were sailing out of New York to the St. Lawrence River, calling at Bar Harbor, Halifax, Saguenay Fjord, Montreal, Quebec and Sydney. These cruises were pretty uneventful except when the seas were rough. I was with friends in Montreal, Canada, enjoying the fall air and the bustling life of the city. We stopped at an old-fashioned ice cream parlor where I opted for my favorite chocolate mint-double scoop in a cone. Four of us strolled along, cones in hand, when I glanced at my watch; the ship was sailing in twenty minutes. I turned backwards to warn the others that we were in trouble and dangerously close to missing the ship. As I turned around to start running I ran smack into a pole, smashed the ice cream in my face and knocked myself out cold. Believe it or not, the others started rubbing their ice cream in my face in order to bring me around. I came to and starting running. As I ran, I tried to wipe the ice cream off my face with my fingers. This made a sticky mess. We made it to the gangway five minutes before sailing. The Staff Captain was mad, until he saw my face. We all explained what happened and I got a warning not to repeat the performance. I never ate ice cream in Montreal again.

We were going out for lunch in the old city of Quebec. The restaurants are many and picturesque. When we chose a particular restaurant, I felt an eerie sensation and I told my friends I could not stay there. It looked very rustic and authentic but I just could not stay there. Everyone followed me outside thinking that I flipped my lid. We went down an alley way to another place and enjoyed some fantastic fish. On the way back, we passed the place I would not go in: it was on fire. I vowed never to go against my instincts; once again they did not fail me.

Rio de Janeiro was the place. Carnival time; insanity time. Six of us stripped off our watches and jewelry, made pockets in our underwear for our money, and told the cab driver, "Impanema Beach". The air was hot and steamy and all the people seemed to be suspended in time. After several hours of loud music, crazy dancing and getting hit on, we were tired but unwilling to leave. We continued to take pictures, walk along the sea wall and enjoy the crowd. Suddenly, three of us were stripped of our clothing. To this day, I do not know how they did it. Our blouses were yanked and gone. Incredibly, they also relieved me of my shorts. The thieves ran, probably thinking our money was in our outside pockets. Surprise! No shops were open to purchase clothing and those on the streets had less on than we. We took a cab back to the ship. Those with clothes tried to cover us while walking on but it was hopeless. The gangway officer had eyes. We explained what happened and ran to our cabins. It was open season on us for following two weeks.

Patrizia Morelli-Pagiatis and I were a team. She was Shore Excursion Manager and I was the Assistant Cruise Director and Port Lecturer on board a seven hundred passenger ship. We did our informational talks together to keep them more interesting. I loved to play jokes on her. We had to give four talks on the first night of embarkation because the first port of call was a next day early morning arrival. She asked me to make my segment of the talk a little longer than usual. She was overworked, frustrated and needed time. I asked the audience to give her a standing ovation when I introduced her because she was voted the best Shore Excursion Manager on the high seas. I quoted the latest ship trade magazines as the source. When she came out, she was stunned by the ovation but did not know why until passengers told her they were privileged to be on the ship with her. When she married, I told everyone she was on her honeymoon and working. Everyone stood and screamed out congratulations and wishes for a happy honeymoon. She turned red. All week everyone asked how the honeymoon was going and she HAD to answer them.

Often we had trouble keeping people away from the gangways while we prepared for arrival in a port. I explained to all that in Antigua, especially, the authorities did not want people crowding the gangway. If this happened, they would delay disembarkation. So I invited everyone to the deck to listen to the steel drum band and to witness Patrizia's dog welcoming her to the island. A stray dog never failed to wait for Patrizia. It would escort her to the taxis as she loaded passengers into them, then escort her back to the ship. The first time I told this story, everyone came out on the deck to film the event. When we arrived, the dog was waiting and ran up the gangway to meet her. The two walked down the gangway and when they reached the concrete, the dog jumped up leaving great muddy paw patterns on Patrizia's starched white skirt. We were in hysterics and hundreds of passengers left with souvenir photos.

Gerry was one of our Cruise Directors. He had a very pleasant singing voice. He was funny and kind and his jokes appealed to all. I volunteered to do a comedy act with him for his show. He was worried but okayed it. I'm 5'6.5" and 120 pounds. He was 6' 6" and more than double my weight. While he sang "Embraceable You", I was to come out on stage telling him that he was boring and needed to put more emotion in his song. After three tries I wasn't happy, so, I made him put his hands behind his back. I stood behind him putting my arms through the loops of his and now becoming his arms. The passengers howled because of the huge contrast between his body and my arms. Each time we did the act, I would pull a different stunt just to keep Gerry on his toes. Once, I brought a razor with shaving cream in my pockets. I sprayed on the cream and pretended to shave his face while he was singing. Of course it appeared that he was doing it to himself. I then straightened his pants and pretended to unbutton them so he could get more relaxed. The audience always laughed. One particular audience laughed louder and longer than any other. When Gerry came off the stage, I discovered the reason for the audience response. The razor's safety cap evidently fell off and I had really shaved the Cruise Director. I wanted to die. I could have cut him badly but I had made zebra stripes in his five o'clock shadow. I chose my stage props more wisely from then on. The next time, I made a small water balloon and attempted to put it in his pants, however, it broke while still in my pocket. Because I was behind Gerry, it looked as if he was wetting his pants and it was streaming down and through the legs all over his shoes. Some in the audience thought he truly let go. I loved it.

We were preparing for a 47-day cruise around South America. My friend Lynda and I went shopping at a popular department store to get all the things we would need. We overbought on the theory that "You never know". We tried on hats - as many as there were. As soon as we put one back, we tried on another. We took all our purchases to the counter, paid for them, got in the car and left. As we were driving, Lynda and I looked at each other and screamed; she still had the hat on. What to do now? The hat was only a few dollars, so we drove on, embarrassed but innocent of premeditated theft. Why the checkout girls never questioned a large store tag hanging from a customer's hat is still a puzzlement.

As a seagoing team, we pinch hit. As a seagoing team, we also played jokes on each other. One time, I decided it was payback time for Katy, a dancer. I organized the staff to have her in the lounge when I started the talent show. She was in the corner talking away. I explained to the audience how the various staff members liked to try something new. I added that it made a department head look better when the staff was diverse in their talents. I called Katy to the stage without giving her advance warning. I told her a little birdie told me that she wanted to MC the talent show just to see what it was like. I handed her the mike and away she went. She had control of the audience in seconds. I was happily shocked when I saw myself doing my own routine. She did a perfect "Joyce": all my jokes, all my mannerisms She got a standing ovation. I bought a round of drinks for everyone.

At one time we were responsible to produce all the decorations for all holidays and special events. The dining room staff saved us time by pitching in to do their own. It was a chore no one enjoyed and we rushed to get it over with. One year, Karen and Tony De Cap came up with the idea to hand make all our Christmas decorations two months previous. It was a great success. We collected dead branches from ashore, painted them white on the back deck of the ship and also made a colossal mess of the deck and ourselves. We strung Styrofoam noodles together to create snow. Crepe paper was used to make door reefs. We bought Santa's elves and sleighs to paint and dress. Karen made a paper mache snowman. A cardboard fireplace was created. A globe was made with pins marking every country represented by the crew. We painted a mural of a snowy village of gleeful mice playing in the fields, sliding on their toboggans and skating on the pond. Tony made a mechanical Santa in a sleigh that flew along the wall. The senior officers received Christmas stockings. It was a home away from home holiday and the spirit of Christmas was everywhere on board. We basked in the warmth of the compliments we received from the passengers. The Captain gave us a private party in his office of champagne and Italian Bacci chocolates. The champagne had its effect after a while. We all laughed at how the Staff Captain was going to reprimand us for drinking when he was keeping up with us. He promised to do just that if we continued drinking once we left the Captain's office. We then named him, "Staff Captain on Wheels". We all pictured him as the old man on the bicycle who keeled over continuously on television's "Laugh In". The Staff Captain was not pleased with us. We left the party quietly and collapsed with laughter once outside the office. Every time he appeared, it set us off into hysterical laughter.

Our decorating duties increased with time. One of the Captains wanted us to blow up hundreds of balloons, string them together and put them along the gangway to liven up the embarkation area. We were not pleased. Turnover time was difficult enough without adding another two hours on a day that ended after midnight and started at six in the morning. The Cruise Director came up with the idea to ask each departing passenger to blow up two balloons to help us celebrate for the Captain's birthday the next morning. Everyone was delighted to help. All we had to do was collect them and string them together. YES.

On the Britanis, our Staff cabins were just above the bridge, similar to a loft in a house. We had to walk up a ladder from inside the officers' quarters to get to our cabins. The deck in the front of them was actually the whole top of the bridge. This area was a favorite of a dancer who seemed to have boundless energy and a homing instinct for the bridge. She enjoyed meeting men to have a good time outside on deck in full view of the Cruise Director's portholes and mine, not to mention the roof of the bridge. We informed her several times that this had to stop. She would not listen. Finally, the Cruise Director and I poured two large champagne buckets full of ice on her and her man. This cooled things off permanently.

At disembarkation we discovered that a passenger was missing. We checked every crew cabin on the theory that he had met a crew member. He had: one of our dancers, only they went to his cabin and never left. We finally made an announcement through the speakers requesting him to check in with Immigration and Customs. He came in fear and the girl ran to her cabin. We had to physically hold our hands over our mouth as Immigration stated that 'it was obvious he was not enjoying his cruise.' Ouch again!

A funny thing happens when any of us goes home for vacation. While we are out shopping for groceries or in a department store, we find ourselves telling people 'hello' in the aisle, or telling them to 'have a nice day', or ask 'if they are having a good time'. The response is usually a look of 'you are a weird person', or we are asked 'if something is the matter with us', or they walk away very quickly. You know, to be friendly is not a bad thing. But this job has us so conditioned we do not know any better. Well, why should we, this is how people should be.

I had a blonde moment in time when I took a taxi to a friend's house in Greece. I was not thinking clearly about the rate of exchange. I read the meter owing 1,700 drachmas; I handed the driver 7,000 drachmas and got out. After visiting with my friend for a couple of hours, I suddenly realized what I had done. I gave the driver about $90.00 for a $10.00 trip and that bugger never said a thing. Typical. Embarrassing.

One summer that my husband and I were off the ship, we had gone spear fishing in the rain. There was thunder and lightening, though I was nervous, I did have on a wetsuit. I borrowed a cap from my husband, the water was so cold. About ten minutes out, I began having mask trouble. Frustrated, I told Iordanis that I would go back to shore, sit in the car and read. After about four hours, Iordanis returned. I looked in the mirror to straighten myself out when I noticed that my hair had a yellowish green hue from the top down the back. I showed Iordanis. He was astonished and could not imagine what had happened. We went back to the house. I washed my hair using an entire bottle of shampoo. The color did not wash out. I then tried lemon juice, hydrogen peroxide and beer. The color did not wash out. After a great deal of thought, Iordanis figured it out. Divers at one time used a chemical called "blue stone". It is mixed with water and squirted into holes where octopus hide to lure them out. My husband uses this when he dives. Somehow the blue stone got into the cap I borrowed and damaged my hair.

I went to a cousin's hairdressing salon. They used a color removal solution. My hair curled and burned. The final solution was to cut my hair off to one inch from my head. What did I feel? Upset. What could I do about it? Nothing. It grew back and life moves on.

One day in the dining room, I was eating a French Dip sandwich. I was down to the last two bites, when my eyes focused on a pair of antennae. Eck! I pulled the sandwich away from my face and inside was the head of a cooked cockroach. I spit out what was in my mouth, revolted at the thought of where the rest of the body was. I called for the Maitre'D and the Chef. When the Chef saw it, he grabbed it and put it in his pocket. His face was beet red as he turned and marched out of the dining room. I could not eat bread for six months after that.

One day on the Antiquity cruise, Lena, the Cruise Director from Greece, announced that it was sprinkling in Nafplio; everyone on the tour should prepare for it. Sixty passengers, all with life jackets, appeared, led by Professor Andronikos. I was puzzled. Was there an emergency that we did not know about? I asked the professor why he had his life jacket on. He told me about the announcement. I called Lena to ask why the passengers needed life jackets for a tour. She said, "No, dear, I told them to bring along a light jacket." The Professor and his group left for the cabins and returned with their light jackets. It was a sweet moment.

During one of the shows, our singer was really into her number. She was to whip off her jacket exposing a very sexy dress. She whipped off the outfit with such force that it flew into the air and landed on a light fixture on the ceiling. We roared. During her number she tried everything to coax it down. The dancers danced around it, repeatedly reaching up to pull it down but it was stuck. The Stage Manager, Lynda, cut the lights after the number and the comedian and male singer went out on the blackened stage and tugged on the jacket. After five minutes of yanking with background mumbling from the pair, it was freed. The show continued with a good amount of fabric still hanging from the lights.

In Greece one summer, we took a dinghy to a private beach. Iordanis went spear fishing. I remained to sun. There were so many bees around, I could not keep them off of me. I jumped in the water and swam over to the dinghy. When I was sitting inside, I looked out over the water and saw what looked like a colossal sized stingray flying across the water. Seconds later, it was gone, leaving rippling water in its wake. I thought I was hallucinating from my fear of all the bees. Until ten minutes later, there were four other boats surrounding the area where "it" went down in the water. I knew then that I was not the only one who saw this strange phenomenon. It never resurfaced. Every time I pass this area, I wonder what it was and will never know. When I explained what I had seen to Iordanis, he gave me a peculiar look.

Sticks and stones are less dangerous than words I was given fifteen minutes to gather my belongings to transfer to another ship. I was displeased but had to go. The Captain got the same transfer order. A staff member warned me that the Captain was spreading a rumor that he had had an affair with me. I arrived on the new ship to see the owner, the Port Captain from ashore and the Captain. I walked right up to him and whispered, "I hear we had an affair, let's get together and talk about it. *Somehow I missed it along the way.*" He looked at me stunned. I felt a chill go through my nerves. That evening he called me up to explain my words. When I told him, he started laughing. He said that the rumor must have come from his cabin steward; that he did not say that he had an affair with me; but that others were saying they would like to have an affair with me. Yes; another blonde moment. I apologized, tucked in my pride and quietly walked out.

From that moment, every time I boarded a vessel I discussed with the staff the subject of hearing and starting rumors. I wrote a sentence on a piece of paper. I folded it, placing it in the center of the table. I whispered the sentence to the closest person to me having each person pass on what they heard to the next. When it came back to me, not one word was in the sentence. Eighteen people heard information. The staff was surprised. We did not start gossip, we spoke directly with the source. At least we tried.

Abuse is not always land based. I one day watched an elderly couple who really did not seem to like each other. Every time this man's wife said anything he did not like, he would hit her over the head with his cane. The first time I saw this, I screeched but I was told to look away. How? This was in public. The third time he did this, I went over, grabbed his cane and threatened to hit him with it if he did it again. He had caused the back of her head to bleed. Who did he think he was to do this to another human being. His wife cried. He told me it was none of my business. I told him that if it was in front of me, it was my business. It sickened me to see this act of violence. He proclaimed his wife was his object to deal with as he pleased. All of the crew was stunned but since this couple was American, they were afraid to do anything. I, however, threatened to turn him over to the police upon arrival in port. He ceased immediately. For the rest of the cruise he remained aloof, bitter and distant, yet did not hit her again. I shudder to think about what happened at home after the cruise.

Abuse is not always obvious. She was beautiful - a Lynda Evans look alike. He was tall and attractive. She had fallen on the gangway in Barbados. When the doctor lifted her skirt to put her in the wheelchair, he saw that her knees were badly bruised and possibly dislocated. He sent her to the local hospital immediately. He was surprised at the extent of her injuries because she had only fallen on the last two steps of the gangway. She arrived back on board, her knees bandaged with orders to stay off her feet until she saw her doctor at home.

Three days later we were in our last port of call before disembarkation. She had fallen out of the top bunk of her cabin and injured her face. Strange? Yes. We were all wondering why her husband made her sleep on the top bunk when her knees were injured. Patrizia, Agnes and I were walking back from town when the taxi arrived bringing this woman back from the local hospital. We went over offering our services; as she turned around, all three of us clasped our mouths stifling horrified gasps. Her face was completely deformed. It seemed the whole left side of her face was sagging down to her feet. It was the most hideous violet plum color I have ever seen. I walked right over to her husband. I whispered that he was disgusting and these so called accidental injuries were excuses to cover up his brutality. I told him that he should be publicly disgraced for his deplorable treatment of a fellow human being. He told me to shut my trap; that he loved his wife. I spit on him and walked away. I pray every day for these two women and others like them.

I suffered from classic migraines. The doctor prescribed morphine and darvon. I had a busy lecture schedule so I went to the doctor for a prophylactic shot. I remember doing the lecture but I was floating above the audience. After the talk, the staff found me on the floor of the dressing room under the costumes with my head along the cool metal wall. I giggled myself silly. They told me I delivered an excellent speech. I did not remember ending it. With the help of the staff I finished off the 'Intro-duction Show' and was taken to my cabin. From then on, I found an holistic way of dealing with my migraines.

The subject of recreational drugs or alcohol is a constant problem. Some crew may decide a ship would be a good place to begin using. The crew is subject to random testing for drugs and alcohol. If drugs are found, justice is swift. If the alcohol level is too high, immediate dismissal is in order. The strictest control is exercised and the crew is made aware of the consequences of violation. A passenger can also be disembarked for behavior that threatens the comfort or safety of others.

Pop went the anchor. In Grand Cayman the ship was anchored outside the harbor because of space limitations. The anchor went down to secure our position. The anchor landed at the edge of an underwater cliff. The rest of the anchor chain draped itself down the side of the cliff. When the current pushed the ship farther away from the anchored position, the anchor fell off the edge of the cliff through the bight in the chain, tying a knot in it. When the anchor was hoisted up the knot tightened. Time for a major pow-wow and serious thinking. A boat was lowered to the chain. The chain was lowered onto the boat while sailors cut off a link, untied the knot and welded the chain back together. The anchor could now finish its path to rest.

In a rare quiet moment, I wrote out the word 'ship-life' trying to come up with what it means for me. I came up with:

(S)eafaring wanderers
(H)aving the courage to face an
(I)tinerary filled with
(P)light.
-
(L)iving
(I)nfamously
(F)or
(E)verlasting memories.

Chapter Eleven
Next Deck, Please

Why a ship is a she? "Because she needs a lot of men to handle her." That is the universal answer of every Captain, including my husband. Anon has even more reasons:

Why a Ship is a She!
A ship is called a SHE because:
There's always a great deal of bustle about her.
There's usually a gang of men arousing her.
It's not the initial expense that breaks you, it's the upkeep.
She's all decked out.
It takes a good man to handle her right.
She knows her topsides, hides her bottom and when coming into port, always heads for the buoys

I'm glad that a ship is called a she because all the attention surrounds her. I enjoy being the center of attention as most women do. Calling a ship a HE is no compliment. Here are an unknown author's reasons why:

Why a Ship Should be a HE!
It is salty and crusty.
Builds a head of steam and goes nowhere.
Bulges and sags in the middle.
Moans a lot and has joints that crack.
Needs a push, a tug and a tender
Toots its horn in every port
Blows its stack
Often stuck in Bars.
Runs a devious course.
Wallows around when empty.
Slow and sluggish when full

Having defined the gender of the ship, here are some of her decorations explained as well as her measurements, a list of what she keeps in her pantry and how clean she keeps her house: The various flags that are flown over the ship have purpose and an exact meaning. All the flags used on vessels are in agreement with the International Flag code. In the days of sailing ships and long before radio, brightly colored flags flown from the rigging could be seen at long distances to allow communication between ships. Today this code allows vessels of all origins to communicate without a language barrier. There are twenty-six flags that represent each letter of the alphabet. Ten flags represent the numbers 0-9. Three special flags, when in use, duplicate the preceding letter or number 1 answering pennant. There are forty flags in all. Every flag, if used alone, has a separate meaning. An illustration of this is that if the flag for the letter "H" is used, (which is half white/half red) it indicates that the Harbor Pilot is on board. If the flags are used in groups of two, three or four together, they will cover almost any subject. Other than these forty flags there are additional flags flown for the nation of the ship's registry, the nation of the port-of-call and the company's flag. Flags used to decorate the ship when in port, are deliberately arranged not to spell out a message.

What is a nautical mile? It is approximately 6,080 feet or 800 feet longer than the familiar statute mile used on land. Knots are nautical miles per hour. They are the unit used to record the ship's speed.

The details of a vessel are easily accessible: The gross registered tonnage, which is not the actual weight of the vessel but rather its volume, the engine type, length and width, etc. These specifics are in the ship's brochure, the website of the Line as well as on board the vessel. For ships calling at U.S. ports, the CDC (Center for Disease Control) Vessel Sanitation Report will provide information with particular emphasis on food handling. This is presented on a numerical rating system. Some companies include the latest rating of their ships on their website.

What are the provisions needed to supply a seven-day cruise? The average consumption of food and drink on a vessel carrying 2,100 passengers plus 900 crew is:

21,600 pounds of beef
  5,040 pounds of lamb
  3,360 pounds of pork
  2,520 pounds of veal
  1,680 pounds of sausage
  4,200 pounds of chicken and turkey
11,760 pounds of fish

675 pounds of crab
3,250 pounds of lobster
21,500 pounds of fresh vegetables
2,500 pounds of potatoes
16,800 pounds of fresh fruit
2,500 gallons of milk
250 quarts of cream
600 gallons of fresh ice cream
8,650 dozen eggs
4,200 pounds of sugar
2,500 pounds of rice
1,500 pounds of cereal
600 pounds of jelly
1,600 pounds of cookies
42,000 tea bags
30 pounds of herbs & spices
3,400 bottles of assorted wines
3,400 bottles of champagne
200 bottles of gin
290 bottles of vodka
350 bottles of whiskey
150 bottles of rum
45 bottles of sherry
600 bottles of assorted liqueurs
10,100 bottles/cans of beer

Passengers ask us: How many nationalities live on board? Depending on the size of the vessel, from ten to sixty. We can sail with as many as sixty different nationalities of passengers on a cruise. Many walks of life are represented. There is a heavy complement of Americans on most of the cruise ships.

Other than the passengers you meet, do you ever see people you know? Yes. In Barbados in the 80's, I escorted four passengers on a taxi tour of the island. When we came to a tourist site, I saw a woman who looked just like my Aunt Betty in California. I wanted to take a picture of her and send it to my Aunt to show her that her double does exist. At the next site, we drove up just as she was leaving. While her driver was slowly pulling out, my driver talked me into chasing the car to get a picture of the woman. As

I ran, the woman saw me and screamed, "Stop the car, it is my niece." We were stunned. Barbados was a port of call for us. Aunt Betty had come there for a vacation. I took her to visit the ship I was working on. She recognized it as one she had sailed the previous year. Coincidence!

On four occasions at airports in London, New York, Chicago and San Francisco, I have been waiting to board my flight when past passengers have approached, remembering me from their cruise. These reunions also happen on the ships. For those who stay in the business, it is easy to work from one ship to another and one company to another, thus increasing the chances of running into seasoned ship travelers. It makes for warm feelings and stories to exchange.

A good example of this is my editor Mary McFadden and her husband Dr. Bill. We traveled together in 1986 on Sun Line's Halley's Comet cruises, then in the '90's again on board Celebrity's Century, Galaxy and Mercury. Each time we forged a closer and closer relationship until we bonded completely. As a magazine writer, editor and tutor of grammar and composition, Mary is well qualified for editorial sea duty. Her love of ships, respect for them and those who sail them gives her a crow's nest vantage point. Bill and Mary are well traveled and good sailors who got their sea legs many years ago. Without a mutual background, especially on the Greek ships, we would have never met. She edited this book by telephone, the Internet, and listening to me as we sailed together. I'm indebted to her for babysitting with my words and changing their verbs when necessary. She tells me she is indebted to me for allowing her to relive every sailing.

Two other devoted passengers are George and Virginia McNamara. The crew is the reason for their continuing voyages. Several crew members have entrusted them with their secrets, their families and their lives. The crew, including me, call them regularly to inform them of the next ship, the next itinerary and the latest episode in the saga of life at sea. The ship is their mind's next door neighbor and they are always visiting in spirit. I had a surprise visit from them in Alaska when they were traveling with another Line for one month. Because they knew where I was, when they got into port, they came over straight away. I had the pleasure of surprising them two weeks later when they did not know we would be in port together again. This is the rotation of fun tales and warm feelings of friendship.

161

Marcelino and Anna Abello are two rare gems from Argentina who are a precious addition to our seagoing family. They have enriched Celebrity Cruise Line vessels on each of their fifty-four cruises and brought on board a sense of style and elegance and glamour that never fails to turn heads wherever they appear.

There is a seagoing family portrait I always carry with me in my mind: Willy Feltman and Jerry Widholm, have passed on. Their fellow Cruise Diectors, Tommy Van (Tilburgh), Paul Franki and Gerry Keating made life at sea a minute-to-minute adventure story. Odysseas and Denise Gikas, Nikos and Patrizia Morelli-Pagiatis and Lynne Domm-Varsamis complete the picture and are permanently in my loving thoughts.

What ships have you and your husband worked on?

Well, for me, they are: SS Stella Solaris, SS Stella Oceanis, SS Stella Maris, Discovery, The MV Victoria, The SS Britanis, The SS Amerikanis, The MV Azur (not worked, traveled with my husband), The MV Horizon.

For Iordanis they are: Adele, Georgia, Delphic Sky, Delphic Eagle, Capetan Karras, Kimon, SS Queen Frederica, SS Patris, Athansios, MV Dalphne, SS Ocean Princess, The SS Victoria, The SS Britanis, The SS Amerikanis, The SS Azur, MV Zenith, MV Horizon, SS Meridian, MV Century, MV Galaxy, MV Mercury and Millennium. Since we meet on the Britanis in 1990, we have traveled together ever since.

Here is an excerpt that was once printed in one of our ships' daily program. This added a little zing to our daily readings and some amusement in our Captains' daily lives:

The Function of a Captain

As nearly everyone knows, A Captain has practically nothing to do except to decide what is to be done.
To tell someone to do it.
To listen to reasons why it should not be done, why it should be done by someone else, or why it should be done in a different way.
To follow up and see if it has been done.
To discover it has not been done.
To inquire why.

To listen to excuses from the person who should have done it.

To follow up again and to see if the thing has been done, only to discover that this time it has been done incorrectly.

To point out how it should be done.

To conclude that as long as it has to be done, it may also be left where it is.

To wonder if it is not time to get rid of a person who cannot do anything right.

To reflect that he probably has a wife and a large family, and that certainly any successor would be just as bad and maybe even worse.

To consider how much simpler and better the thing would have been done if one had done it oneself in the first place.

To reflect sadly that one could have done it right in 20 minutes, and, as things turned out, one had to spend two days to find out why it took three weeks for somebody else to do it wrong.

Author Unknown

Does your time on board allow any sort of "normal" life? Well, yes and no. Many of us have gotten off the ships to make a family, some of us have stayed on while making a family and some have retired with a family. Over the past twenty years with those I still keep in contact with, we have 42 children and 18 grandchildren among us.

During my years of collecting the material to write our memoirs, I added a chapter on motherhood. There were miscarriages and the heartaches following for both Iordanis and me. At midnight on February 24, 1997, I diagnosed myself as having gas pains from too many shrimp hours before. My mother diagnosed me as being in labor. At 2:30 A.M., my beloved Dr. Pepas agreed with my mother. He calmly but definitively announced that we must get to the hospital; the baby is on its way home. The streets were empty, yet it took us one and half hours to get to the hospital. Though we could see the hospital clearly in the distance, the road to get to it would not open its arms. With my mother and father each holding one of my hands, we circled and circled again. This took fifteen minutes each time. I screamed every cuss word I knew in every language trying to get Iordanis to go through the red lights and turn where I told him to turn. When we finally arrived, the hospital personnel were waiting. I marked my territory by vomiting on the entrance and arrived at the door hunched over. Once inside I was very well cared for. I was still using my working diagnosis of gas pains. All would be well if I could just be directed to the bathroom. Neh, neh (the Greek "yes") I heard but both my diagnosis and my requests were ignored. I insisted in Greek and English, accompanied by a small tantrum. They finally let me go and I was fine. Suddenly the doctor said, "Take her in, it is time." I arrived in the delivery room at 5:50A.M. Haris (Haralampos) Adamidis arrived 6:10A.M. introducing himself to his father and mother clearly and sweetly. The minute we looked at him, we could never imagine what our lives were like without him. What we had never learned from our travels, we have now learned from him. Haris challenges us with a new learning process every day.

Haris started his ship travels with us at six weeks. In his short three and half years of life, he has been in 15 countries and has played with children of all races and nations. Even now, in the ship's playroom, he gravitates to those who do not speak English, taking them by the hand and being their friend. He is a tiny ambassador to the countries of the world that speak "children." Through him and millions like him, tolerance of each other might possibly rise from the ashes of prejudice. Our goal and dream is to give him a brother or sister and for Iordanis to retire for the enjoyment of sharing our lives together.

How do you communicate with someone when you do not speak his or her language?

There are a number of ways. Most importantly with a big smile; a smile travels a long way. Then you hold hands mentally, you try to try and then you always leave them laughing. Laura Carboni, an Italian, one of our boutique girls, is a perfect example of this type of diplomacy. A German man, with probably three extra beers aboard, was trying on an extra large t-shirt. It did not fit but the shop did not carry extra-extra large. Laura held up another extra large shirt to him and he decided to try it. She looked at him and said,' Naa, gutt, gutt'. The man bought the shirt and left happy. Laura turned to me and said, "See, sometimes, though it is marked one way, it still might be slightly larger. So why not have him try it, if he likes it, then he buys it. I try to say yes and no in any language to let them know I am trying. A few days later, a French woman came in. The conversation with Laura sounded like this (phonetically), "Bon jour madame." "Bon jour madame." "Blah blah blah blah." "Oh, no we?" "Blah blah blah blah, no madame." "Ah we!" "Ohrevwah", "Ohrevwah, madame."

Laura," I asked, "what were you talking about, I thought you did not speak French". "I don't, but I listened to the tone of her voice and followed her. Just answering yes and no. It really does not matter, he left content."

It is all a matter of making one feel good. We were performing, "If I Were Not Upon The Sea" one night. An elderly Italian man bolted from his theater seat, ran up the stairs to the stage, grabbed me, bent me backwards and kissed me, Roberto Bennini style. Why this spontaneity? He wanted us to know he was having a wonderful time. "Grazie, Signor".

Here is a collection of passenger comments, questions and statements made either to coworkers or to me personally over the years. They have provided, to quote Gilbert and Sullivan, "a source of innocent merriment." It is obvious that a phenomenon is involved here; not unlike the force that seems to overtake some women when they see a man with epaulets. When some passengers board they seem to put their brain in neutral the second the gangway metal becomes carpet. This is okay. This is what the brochure refers to when they promise total care of the passenger - pampering - This is accurate. It is your vacation and your time to be free of all land based problems and duties. It is time to let someone else carry out the cooking, entertaining, running around and answering the phone. Sit back now and read what your fellow passengers asked and still do ask. When the Cruise Director tells some of the following stories at the disembarkation talk, the passengers laugh in disbelief. Believe!

I had heard the first question quoted by numerous Cruise Directors during the years and always thought that they made it up. But then one day, someone really did ask me: "Is the pool filled with seawater?" "Yes." "Oh, so that answers why there are so many waves in it."

Is the ship supposed to move like this or is it an accident?
I have a guaranteed cabin. I think it has an ocean view.
Can I get an inside cabin with a window?
Do we put our luggage outside our door before or after we sleep?
Do you have friends?
Do the crew ever get married?
How much are we allowed to eat?
Do we need to pay for the extra food?
How much is the show?
Do you have to speak another language to speak with the crew?

What do you and the crew do for a living?

Does the crew work on board?

Where is the left balcony in the Theater?

Can I see the cockpit?

How far above sea-level are we?

Why did they not take pictures of the hieroglyphics in the cave in 2000 B.C.? They would have been clearer to see and better preserved if they had.

Is it important to be back on the ship after the tour?

Have you seen my husband? He is fat, bald and with a protruding belly.

(And the other side of the coin), Have you seen my girlfriend? She is short with gray hair.

Can you take the elevator to the front of the ship?

Does it matter what side of the ship we get off on?

Can the telephones be used ashore?

Can the Captain go on the bridge in his pajamas?

What time is the midnight buffet?

What do you do with the ice carvings after they melt?

Do we need to declare the alcohol we purchased from ashore and drank on the ship?

Does the tour bus pick us up in our staterooms?

Will I get wet on the snorkeling tour?

Do we have to get off the ship to meet on the pier?

Does the ship generate its own electricity?

Is it sea water in the toilets?

We had a group of East Germans traveling with us out of the port of Miami. At the end of the cruise one of the passengers wrote on his comment sheet: Too many Americans on board!

And again, the other side of the coin: On the same cruise an American man wrote: Next time tell me that so many East Germans would be on board; then I would not mistake a woman with hairy armpits and flabby tits of being a man next to me by the pool.

Where do all these Chinese passengers come from?

I think we got some fruits that were not for us, but we ate them, are we allowed to keep the bowl?

Why can't we use 911 on board?

Is there a charge for a wake-up call?

Is there a charge to call another cabin?

Is it long distance to call ashore?

Do I have to press 'play' on VCR to see a movie?

Can I book a cruise to Hawaii? But I want to embark in New York.

Do we need to go through customs in every port?

Are we going to capsize in one meter of water?

I was standing by the elevators and stairs one day when a sweet little woman asked me: "Do these stairs work?" I answered with a smile, "No, Ma'am, they are out of order today, you better take the elevator."

As my short memoir has been written, it has been neatly wrapped in this short quotation without much room for debate. It encapsulates who I am and why:

> There are three kinds of people.
> Those that are living,
> Those that are dead,
> And those that are at sea."
>
> By Anarcarchis in the 3rd century B.C.

Iordanis, Haris and I stepped into the ship's elevator one day on deck 5. We were headed for luncheon and on the way up, joined an experiment in international relations. Two Chinese passengers entered on deck 6. We exchanged smiles and greetings. On deck 7, the Chinese couple left and three Indians boarded. We exchanged smiles and greetings. On 8, they left and two Spaniards entered. More smiles! More greetings! We stopped on deck 9, where they left and two French boarded. Again there were greetings and mutual smiles were reflected in the mirrored walls of the elevator. We soon stopped on deck 10 where the Greek Captain Iordanis, our son Haris, who is half Greek and half American along with me, the all American, left and the others continued. With Haris in hand and following Iordanis, I smiled saying, "Wow, did you see that? We just went around the world in the ship's elevator." I felt honored to have seen all those different faces. I felt united with humanity seeing that we got along so well by just saying "Hi" and smiling at each other. If only we could stretch the smiles and translate "Hi" into every language, we could take the "differ" out of "different".

Although I am used to passengers' questions and accustomed, as well, to figures, I never thought this would come up BUT. I was asked approximately how many passengers have I met during my years at sea Well, the total came to about 785,000 while Iordanis numbers more than one million. We are still counting. Each of these people has given us insight into their mentality, customs, preferences and dislikes. They have taught us to approach problems and their solutions in ways very different from ours. They have taught us to exchange views - either accepting or rejecting them but at least to investigate their culture.

The educational value gleaned from my travels is home based. I thank my parents because they have instilled in my brothers and me the importance of keeping an open mind and to use tolerance as a yardstick to judge all circumstances involving us or our families. There is no better advice than this.

A ship carries its own spectrum of colors - colors that represent nationalities, folkways and mores. Every time I saw a rainbow at sea, I always felt it was nature agreeing with me. Ships carry tales within their hull; some to become shared and others to be swallowed by the sea. This book is our gift to our children so they can know who we were before they "were."

As the ropes are slowly hoisted up and the anchor tucked away for rest, the ship, in silent unhurried motion, slips away from her berthing place. The sunset explodes rays of color over the horizon, the whistle blows 'bon voyage' and another new cruise is born to sail. As the breeze of the soft sweet sea air brushes our faces, the sounds of past cruises echo in our hearts, the scent of present cruises electrifies our hearts and the esoteric waiting of future cruises is silent in our hearts. Yes, the vessels will continue to change while the people will remain unchanged. It is the new generation that will hear the stories of the past, live the stories of the present and will preserve the stories for the future.

There is a mystique about the sea that heightens and intensifies emotions. A ship at sea is mildly mind altering. From the moment the lines are slipped, the great escape begins and people react to freedom change, the unknown and the luxury of being cared for instead of caring for.

One of the most fascinating sentences I have ever read, was written by Karl Husman in his book, "Against the Grain." He wrote: "The pleasure of travel only exists, as a matter of fact, in retrospect and seldom in the present at the instant when it is being experienced."

If I were not upon the sea
a roving anchor I would be.
I'd catch each ship that passed me by
and haul it towards me
so that I
could board and happy be
to once again be on the sea

About the Author:

When she left her native California 20 years ago, Joyce Gleeson ran away to sea and signed on to cruise ships. There she wore many name tags; variously identifying her as "Social Hostess", "On Board Lecturer", "Assistant Cruise Director" and "Cruise Director".

Some years ago, she added "Captain's Wife" to her titles and "Adamidis" to her passport when she married a handsome Greek Captain. Their son is amphibious and owned a tuxedo (for formal nights on board) before he could walk.

When she is land based, it is either in Mariposa, California or Piraeus, Greece.